The Interdisciplinary Study of Politics

MONTE PALMER
The Florida State University

LARRY STERN
Mars Hill College

CHARLES GAILE
The Florida State University

Harper & Row, Publishers
New York, Evanston, San Francisco, London

Sponsoring Editor: Ronald Taylor
Project Editor: William B. Monroe
Production Supervisor: Bernice Krawczyk

The Interdisciplinary Study of Politics
Copyright © 1974 by Monte Palmer, Larry Stern, and Charles Gaile
All rights reserved. Printed in the United States of America. No part of
this book may be used or reproduced in any manner whatsoever without
written permission except in the case of brief quotations embodied in
critical articles and reviews. For information address Harper & Row,
Publishers, Inc., 10 East 53rd Street, New York, N.Y. 10022.

Library of Congress Cataloging in Publication Data

Palmer, Monte.
    The interdisciplinary study of politics.

    Includes bibliographical references.
    1. Political science. 2. Social sciences.
I. Stern, Larry, joint author. II. Gaile, Charles,
joint author. III. Title.   *CIP 23 79*
JA71.P333   301.5'92   74-7097
ISBN 0-06-044975-6

to
Charles Gaile, Sr.

Contents

Preface   ix

1. **Conceptual Analysis   1**
    Concepts and Constructs   4
    Hypotheses   6
    Theory   6
    Conceptual Frameworks   9
    Models   10
    The Evaluation on Concepts   11
    An Organizational Note   16

2. **General Social Science Concepts   19**
    Systems Analysis   19
    Supports   21
    Power   25
    Communications   33
    Critique   41

3. **Some Concepts of Sociology   44**
    Social Structure   44
    Role   45
    Groups   48
    Social Stratification   54
    Function   59
    The Structural–Functional Analysis of Political Systems   64
    Summary   71

4. Anthropology and Politics   75
Primitive Societies   76
Culture   92
The Political Relevance of Culture: Political Culture and
   National Character   95
Critique   100

5. Economics and Politics   106
Decision Making: The Rational Model   107
Resources   113
Exchanges   115
Costs   118
Bargaining   119
Coalitions   123
The Theory of Games   125
Spatial Modeling   131
Critique   132

6. Psychology and Politics   137
Some Necessary Background   139
Politics and Need–Based Psychology   142
Identity and Identification   147
Frustration–Aggression   154
Efficacy   156
Perception, Cognition, and the Formation of Political
   Attitudes   157
Decision Making   161
Operant Conditioning as an Approach to Political Learning   164
Critique: Psychology of Politics   167

Index   173

Preface

In the years since the end of World War II the discipline of political science has experienced a behavioral revolution and a quantitative revolution. Many behaviorally oriented political scientists have also stressed quantitative research techniques, and a tendency has arisen to use the two terms interchangeably; however, they are not interchangeable. Quantification refers to the numbering, counting, and statistical manipulation of data, regardless of its nature. The term "behavior" refers to a specific type of data—human behavior—and to concepts relating to human behavior.

Considerable agreement now exists among political and social scientists concerning the appropriate statistical usage for various types of political analyses. Excellent manuals of instructions are available at all levels of sophistication, and computer packages such as the *Statistical Package for the Social Sciences* make a variety of complex statistical techniques available to political scientists with only moderate statistical skills.

The behavioral revolution has produced no such uniformity. Behavioral concepts, often poorly defined, are applied in a multitude of ways with little reference to their application in other political science literature or in the literature of the social sciences in general. Furthermore, few works exist to provide the student with a critical introduction to the origins, applicability, and limitations of the broad range of behavioral concepts now widely used in political analysis. In *The Interdisciplinary Study of Politics* we hope to take a small step toward meeting this need. Specifically, we want to introduce the student to the vast and tantalizing array of behavioral concepts available to the political analyst, to illustrate their use by political scientists as well as by members of other social science disciplines, and to critique their weaknesses and analytical limitations. The book also serves as a minimal source of reference for students unfamiliar with or confused by the use of behavioral concepts in the political science literature.

Writing this book has not been an easy task. Some behavioral concepts possess literally hundreds of definitions within their discipline of origin, not to mention their use by political scientists. The concept "personality," for example, is said to have more than 400 definitions. We have plagued colleagues in all social science disciplines with demands for clarification and advice. All, far too numerous to mention, have given freely of their time and expertise. The definitions thus provided reflect this advice and are, in our best judgment, the prevailing usage of the concept in the discipline of its origin. We have endeavored to offer definitions that are as clear and precise as possible. The inherent ambiguity of many concepts renders precision impossible, however, and in certain cases we have noted both the existence of ambiguity and its sources. We, of course, accept full responsibility for the book and its contents.

We wish to thank Laura Cortese and Rebecca Dorsett for their efficient and accurate typing of the manuscript.

M. P.
L. S.
C. G.

The
Interdisciplinary
Study of Politics

Conceptual Analysis

The goal of political science is to systematically explain and predict political phenomena. Therefore, political scientists often must be in a position to analyze the broad spectrum of factors that influence human behavior, even though many of these factors may seem to be far removed from the traditional realm of politics.

For example, one could hardly explain the complexities of political decision making without also considering such psychological variables as the values, prejudices, idiosyncrasies, and other personality traits that influence the manner in which the decision maker perceives his universe and his role within that universe. Also relevant would be the pressures and constraints emanating from the decision maker's social, cultural, and economic milieu. Indeed, Marxist-oriented analysts would argue that knowledge of economics is a precondition for the analysis of political decision making.

Similarly, the analysis of political phenomena such as public opinion or nationalism soon leads the political scientist into the study of the formation of basic attitudes and loyalties. This in turn necessitates the study of personality development, learning theory, socialization, and social stratification, as well as a host of other variables.

It is difficult, then, to study political behavior without reference to the social, economic, cultural, and psychological milieu in which it occurs.

This does not mean that all aspects of an individual's milieu are relevant to his political behavior. The determination of the aspects of human behavior and environment that are relevant, as well as the circumstances under which they are or are not relevant, however, is part and parcel of political science. Thus the boundaries of political science merge with the disciplines of sociology, psychology, anthropology, and economics. In the years to come, there is every indication that they will also merge with biology and physiology which, in conjunction with the fields named, are now referred to as the behavioral sciences. Therefore, unless political scientists become sufficiently familiar with the concepts and techniques of the other behavioral sciences to enable them to utilize such concepts, techniques, and findings in the analysis of political phenomena, they will be unable to either draw on or contribute to the growing body of integrated behavioral knowledge.

Also, if political scientists are to explain and predict political phenomena, and if the "science" in political science is not to be a total misnomer, it is essential that the research of political scientists increasingly observe the rigors of the scientific method.[1] Thus, among other things, they must define their terms and concepts to provide specific, uniform meanings throughout the discipline. This is a particularly burdensome requirement for political scientists, for most of the key words in our vocabulary are anything but specific. If ten political scientists are asked to spell out precisely what they mean by the concept of "power," they will more than likely provide ten distinct answers. Nevertheless, the term "power" continues to be used as if both its meaning and implications were universally clear.

A second requirement of the scientific method is that research be cast in the form of empirically testable hypotheses —that is, that hypotheses be testable by sensory (observable) data. Thus in the scientific method such metaphysical concepts as God or natural law are unsuitable for explaining political phenomena because the existence of the things conceptualized must be accepted as a matter of faith: It cannot be observed or measured by means of the human senses.

A third requirement of the scientific method—replicability —necessitates the stating of propositions in empirical terms and the establishment of specific definitions. To the greatest extent possible, other researchers must be able to perform the same research and to ascertain for themselves the validity of our conclusions.

The importance of the requirement of replicability is difficult to exaggerate. The research of any one individual is naturally subject to errors of design, errors of execution, and errors of data interpretation. The more research leading to important findings is replicated, the greater confidence one can place in the validity of those findings. Furthermore, the greater confidence a discipline places in the collective work of its members, the greater its ability to expand, refine, and build on those contributions as a means of developing a theory or theories capable of explaining and predicting a growing array of phenomena.

A fourth requirement of the scientific method is that research be free of the bias of the researcher's personal values. The question of values is clearly one of the most perplexing problems the social scientist must face. Both logically and empirically it is impossible for human beings to totally insulate their research from values. In selecting a research problem, for instance, a value preference is reflected in the very act of choosing one subject over another. In choosing collaborators for complex research projects, value preferences again enter the picture. The same is true when we decide how much time to allocate to the search for empirical data, and this decision may even influence the rigor of our evaluative standards. Researchers often "squeeze blood out of a turnip" to make their findings seem important.

It is incumbent on the political scientist to be as rigorous as possible in eliminating from his research design and testing processes values that are likely to bias his results. Many researchers attempt to facilitate this process by making their own value position explicit. However, one's inability to be totally rigorous in this regard makes it even more important that our research be conducted in ways that can be easily replicated by others.

Is science enough? Few political scientists would deny the need for greater rigor in political research or the desirability of a science of politics. However, many political scientists—perhaps a majority—would argue that being scientific is not enough. Their view, and it is a very telling one, is that political science must be relevant to the urgent crises confronting American society and the world at large. Let us state the argument in its strongest form: What good is a science of politics that ignores urban chaos, the proliferation of thermonuclear weapons, overpopulation, starvation, racial bigotry, ecological disaster, genocide in Africa and Asia, governmental repression everywhere and, according to some, the gradual disintegration of American society? A profession that ignores the crises of its day is shortsighted, at best.

Yet a gap need not exist between the need for greater relevance and the need for scientific rigor in political research. Quite the contrary; if the scientific method provides the most efficient means for supplying reliable information concerning the origin and perpetuation of social problems, the scientific method also provides the most efficient means to their solution. It does not always tell us clearly what should be studied or how the results should be used—there is no substitute for human values in making these decisions. But goal- or problem-oriented research certainly can be conducted in an empirical manner.

This book introduces the concepts and hypotheses, developed in the fields of sociology, anthropology, economics, and psychology, that relate directly to the analysis of political phenomena, illustrating and critiquing their use by political scientists, as well. The book is not a text of research design, statistics, or methodology. Matters of methodology, however, are difficult to divorce from the study of concepts. To the foregoing comments on the scientific method, we might add that the ability to evaluate the utility of concepts, whether native to political science or adapted from the various social science disciplines, requires a brief discussion of the term *concept* and its relation to other intellectual tools such as *theories*, *conceptual frameworks*, *hypotheses*, and *models*. This done, a checklist for the evaluation of concepts is related to specific methodological considerations.

CONCEPTS AND CONSTRUCTS

In the everyday world individuals are confronted by an endless variety of discreet, one-of-a-kind, phenomena. For example, people speak of President Nixon's first inaugural speech, the steel strike of 1948, the Vietnam War, or the presidential election of 1972. Each is a specific label that has a single, specific, one-of-a-kind empirical referent.

To think effectively, however, an individual must also group discreet events into categories and generalize about their properties. It is difficult to discuss the specific election of 1972, for example, without reference to "elections" as a general category. Similarly, a description of the American electorate would be difficult if each voter had to be considered individually, as would a discussion of the military if each soldier had to be identified as a discreet entity.

To think and communicate effectively, therefore, all human beings sort and classify empirical phenomena on the basis of differences and similarities. That is to say, they conceptualize. Thus one of the most widely accepted definitions of a concept is: "The general ideas which are used for classes of items."[2] A concept might also be defined as any general noun. Power, authority, alienation, influence, development, and change are all common political science concepts.

Concepts are categories or types of behavior, individuals, institutions, actions, beliefs, images, events, places, or virtually anything else. They describe a single category, not relationships between categories. Hypotheses, conceptual frameworks, theories, and models, by way of contrast, are all ways of visualizing or testing relationships between concepts.

Concepts, then, are the subject matter of political analysis. They are the building blocks of hypotheses, models, conceptual frameworks, and theories.

Within the realm of the social sciences, you are likely to encounter three types of concepts: empirical, heuristic, and metaphysical. An *empirical concept* is presumed to exist in the world of our experience; however nebulous or abstract, the (often incorrect) assumption persists that the thing conceptualized can be demonstrated and measured by means of sensory data.

Heuristic concepts are not assumed to exist but are useful for visualizing empirical relationships and guiding research. The physicists concept of a "perfect vacuum" is an example of a heuristic concept. We do not assume that the thing conceived of exists, but it provides a standard against which existing vacuums can be measured. Similarly, anthropologists, sociologists, and economists studying different stages of economic and political development often posit (assume) a scale of societies ranging from an "ideal-type" traditional society to an ideal-type modern society.[3] The ideal types are not presumed to exist, but they are useful for visualizing (empirical) relationships in the real world.

Metaphysical concepts do not have empirical referents; that is, they cannot be established and measured by reference to sensory data, and they are not posited specifically to assist in the conceptualization of empirical relationships.

"God" and "natural law" are metaphysical concepts, not amenable to investigation by means of the scientific method. Their existence and influence must be accepted on faith.

The term *construct* has much in common with the term "concept," but it is one of the more ambiguous terms in political science. To some it means any form of mental abstraction. To others it is a more limited term referring to the most precise and rigorously defined concepts. Still others have assigned the term construct to the most nebulous concepts, such as Freud's concepts of id and super-ego. For present purposes, concepts and constructs are regarded as having essentially the same meaning.

HYPOTHESES

A *hypothesis* is a statement of a suspected relationship between variables that can be empirically tested. Unless variables refer to specific persons, places, or things, variables may be presumed to be concepts. Hypothetical statements are generally cast in an *if–then* format. *If x, then y. If* both parents identify with one party, *then* the probability of their children identifying with the same party is higher than in cases of parents who identify with opposing parties. *If* individuals are prejudiced against one minority group, *then* they are likely to be prejudiced against all minority groups.

To be empirically tested, of course, all concepts and variables used in the hypothesis must be rigorously defined and must refer to empirical phenomena.

A hypothesis that has been tested and substantiated by several scholars in a wide variety of circumstances may eventually be accepted as a theory. Theories in the realm of politics, however, are few and far between. Most political research remains at the level of exploring hypothetical relationships.

THEORY

The term *theory* is used in a variety of ways. Until very recently, the expression "political theory" referred to the discourses of classical philosophers such as Plato, Aristotle, Thomas Hobbes, or Sir Thomas More.

Such theories were generally referred to as *normative theories*, inasmuch as their primary function was to describe or justify an ideal set of political or social relationships. In most instances, they were based on a priori knowledge; that is, the theory was conceived and expounded before the facts relevant to it were available, and the referents used could not be measured empirically. The following excerpt from Hobbes's *Leviathan* illustrates normative theory:

The right of nature, which writers commonly call *jus naturale*, is the liberty each man has to use his own power, as he will himself, for the preservation of his own nature—that is to say, of his own life—and consequently of doing anything which, in his own judgement and reason, he shall conceive to be the aptest means thereunto. . . .

And because the condition of man, as has been declared in the precedent chapter, is a condition of war of every one against everyone—in which case everyone is governed by his own reason and there is nothing he can make use of that may not be a help unto him in preserving his life against his enemies—it follows that in such a condition every man has a right to everything, even to one another's body. And therefore, as long as this natural right of every man to everything endures, there can be no security to any man, how strong or wise soever he be, of living out the time which nature ordinarily allows men to live. And consequently it is a precept or general rule of reason that everyman ought to endeavor peace, as far as he has hope of obtaining it; and when he cannot obtain it, that he may seek and use all helps and advantages of war.[4]

Political scientists also use the term "theory" in a more rigorous empirical sense resembling the use of the term in the physical sciences. Like the hypothesis, the model, and the conceptual framework, the empirical theory is a statement of the manner in which certain specified variables (concepts) relate to other specified variables (concepts), under certain specified conditions.

A hypothesis, however, is a statement of a *suspected* relationship between two or more variables. A theory is an *empirically verified* statement of a relationship between variables.[5] In testing by a wide variety of investigators, the certain specified variables of the hypothesis did relate to certain other specified variables under the certain specified conditions in the predicted manner.

Once a theory has been empirically verified, it can be used to deduce a wide variety of propositions contained within the framework of the theory, which then should also be true.

For example, if Anthony Downs's hypothesis "that political parties in a democracy plan their policies so as to maximize votes" were to receive sufficient empirical verification to accord it theory status, it should be possible to logically deduce the following propositions, which should also be true.

Proposition 1. Party members have as their chief motivation the desire to obtain the intrinsic rewards of holding office; therefore, they formulate policies as means to holding office rather than seeking office in order to carry out preconceived policies. . . .

Proposition 2. Both parties in a two-party system agree on any issues that a majority of citizens strongly favor. . . .

Proposition 6. Democratic governments tend to redistribute income from the rich to the poor. . . .

Proposition 7. Democratic governments tend to favor producers more than consumers in their actions. . . .[6]

If one of these propositions were found to be invalid, either the entire theory would have to be modified to account for the variation, or we would have to reject it. Moreover, the testing of theories and their propositions is an unending process, regardless of how good their past record may be.

An empirical theory emerging from the ever-increasing accumulation of data is referred to as an *inductive theory.* A theory from which empirically testable propositions are deduced is referred to as a *deductive theory.* Most theories emerge by means of induction. Once their credentials have been firmly established, they are used as deductive theories to generate additional testable propositions.

In terms of generality, a theory explaining all political behavior would be clearly superior to a theory that could only explain voting behavior. Working backward, we see that a theory that could only explain voting behavior would be superior to a theory that could only explain voting behavior in the United States. But a theory that could explain voting behavior in the United States clearly would be superior to a theory that could only explain the voting behavior of a single individual or a small group of individuals. Thus the more general the theory, the better.

Unfortunately, the discipline of political science currently lacks the tools to empirically validate the relationship between the myriad concepts influencing political behavior and the conditions under which they may vary. Indeed, political scientists are still grappling with the more basic problem of identifying the diverse variables that may influence political behavior. We are far from achieving the goal of developing a grand theory of politics.

Therefore, political scientists have increasingly turned their attention to middle-range theory and low-range theory, which, as the names imply, refer to theories of limited scope. Downs's hypothesis, if validated, might be an example of middle-range theory. A theory that could only predict or explain the voting behavior of a single individual would be a very low-level theory. Yet if an empirically verified theory could be developed to explain the behavior of a few individuals, it might be carefully extended, modified, and elaborated to explain the behavior of even larger groups. In their efforts at theory building, political scientists have tended to eschew the very real possibility of constructing verifiable low-level theories for the glory and frustration of starting with grand theory and gradually attempting to work their way down.

CONCEPTUAL FRAMEWORKS

A theory, then, is an empirically verified statement specifying how rigorously defined, empirically testable concepts *do* behave under explicitly defined circumstances.

A conceptual framework or analytical framework is a speculative statement of how concepts *might* behave under various circumstances. (The terms "conceptual framework" and "analytical framework" are synonymous.) For example, many psychiatrists and many clinical and social psychologists make extensive use of the concepts of id, ego, super-ego, and other components of the subconscious to explain and predict human behavior. The components of the subconscious cannot be directly observed, and they defy empirical measurement by indirect means. In spite of the difficulties of measurement, such concepts are considered by their adherents, including several political scientists, to be extremely useful in visualizing or conceptualizing what takes place in the individual mind.

Chapter 2 contains an extensive discussion of *systems analysis*, or the view that a direct analogy can be drawn between the operation of mechanical systems such as an automobile and the operation of the political system within a state or society. Although it seems that we are a long way from learning to empirically demonstrate that a direct analogy can be drawn between the political process and a mechanical or biologic system, many political scientists nevertheless find that assuming politics to be a *system* is a very useful way of visualizing the political process and generating hypotheses.

Thus we can think of a conceptual framework as a grand and complex hypothesis. The more rigorously the terms and concepts are defined and the more they lend themselves to empirical verification, the better chance such conceptual frameworks possess of eventually becoming models or theories.

MODELS

Models are simulations of reality—analogies that make the complexities of the real world more easy to visualize. A globe, for example, is a model of the earth that helps geographers in the otherwise difficult task of accurately portraying the interrelationships between the earth's various landmasses and oceans. The more accurately the geographer's globe corresponds to empirical reality, the greater its utility in helping him to describe, predict, and explain geographic phenomena. Political and social scientists have similarly attempted to develop models that would simplify political analysis by indicating the manner in which the various concepts influencing political behavior are interrelated.[7] Within this framework, political science models vary in scope, complexity, and rigor from simple speculative statements "that the behavior of nations can be predicted by assuming that states will always act to maximize their power," through closely reasoned, mathematical models such as those suggested by William H. Riker and William Zavoina.[8]

Given the diverse usage of the term "model" by social scientists, however, it is difficult to differentiate a model from other intellectual tools, such as theories and conceptual frameworks. To some political scientists a model should have all the properties of an empirical theory and, in fact, is merely a synonym for theory.[9] Other social scientists, as the following quotation illustrates, consider any conceptual framework to be a model.

. . . Rapoport contends that the structure of a model need not be extensive at all. Recognizing that, for the social scientist, a "theory is often (in effect) a system of reference, that is, merely a multitude of definitions," he contends that "most models are too simple to fit into the exceedingly involved interplay of variables associated with human behavior." It is sufficient, he says, if an analytic scheme "contains the essentials, no matter how crudely simplified, of some social process." If it does this, it is a model. Levy's position is similar. DeFleur and Larsen similarly assert that the function of a model is "to point out where to look, and under what conditions to make the observations or discriminatory responses." For them, also, a scheme need have little extensiveness of structure to be considered a model.[10]

In analyzing the variety and imprecision with which the term model is used by social scientists, Robert Golembiewski suggests that models should be viewed as an intermediate step between conceptual frameworks and empirical theories.[11] As such, a model would go well beyond a conceptual framework in meeting the requirements of an expirical theory, yet would be less rigorous in meeting the theoretical demands for empirical verification and generality (breadth of application).

This idea has considerable merit, but the term "model" continues to be applied indiscriminately to a wide variety of intellectual formulations, and accordingly it continues to lack precise meaning.

THE EVALUATION OF CONCEPTS

If concepts are the building blocks of hypotheses, theories, conceptual frameworks, and models, it follows that any analytical structure built on concepts can be no stronger, no more accurate, and no more analytically efficient than the concepts on which it is based. The mere fact of placing concepts in a theoretical framework does not improve their inherent quality.

As political analysis has increasingly come to focus on human behavior, political scientists have turned to the other social sciences for conceptual assistance. Indeed, the conceptually rich fields of sociology and psychology seem to provide virtually limitless explanations of political behavior. Much conceptual borrowing, however, has been hasty and indiscriminate. Many borrowed concepts have proved to be less empirically sound than they once appeared to be. Other concepts have been used in ways unintended by their originators. Although it is now essential for political scientists to take an interdisciplinary approach to political analysis, the adapting and applying of borrowed concepts to political analysis must proceed with caution and rigor. Continual testing and reevaluation of concepts is an essential element of the scientific process. The same is true of the evaluation of new political science concepts as well as those whose value has been long established. The following points can be considered to be a starting point in making such evaluations.

Definitional Clarity

Operationalization   Every empirical concept requires two forms of definition—conceptual definition and operational. The *conceptual definition* conveys the content of the concept in written or verbal communication. The *operational definition* specifies how the concept is to be empirically measured. *Economic class* might be defined conceptually as "a social stratum or category differentiated from other such strata on the basis of wealth, occupation, or property." Operationally, social class might be defined on the basis of specific indicators or wealth, occupation, or property. The middle class, for example, might be operationally defined as all families with a yearly income of between $8,000 and $15,000. The results of empirical research, of course, vary markedly depending on how we choose to operationalize our concepts. Middle-class behavior when "middle class" is defined as family income between $8,000 and $15,000 may well be different from middle-class behavior when an annual family income between $6,000 and $25,000 is used. The checklist that follows pertains largely to the conceptual definitions of concepts. The problems of operationalization are complex and are the proper subject of methodology texts. *Any concept used in empirical research, however, must be capable of being operationalized.*

Exclusiveness   A concept is a common noun referring to categories of items, events, actions, and images. Virtually all common nouns in the dictionary are concepts. To effectively communicate information about the influence of one concept on another, such as the impact of religion on political participation or the impact of sex on voting, the conceptual definition of a concept *must refer to only one specific category of phenomena* and should possess a single definition. "Dogs" should refer to "dogs," and there should be but one conceptual definition of dogs. Most social science concepts, however, cannot meet this requirement. The "balance of power" concept has at least six definitions, each one referring to a different category of events and action. The concept of "personality" is reported to have at least 400 conceptual definitions, and the concept of "culture" must have at least that many. The more definitions we have, the more difficult effective communication becomes.

Precision   In the middle ages, philosophers debated mightily over the properties of phlogiston, the supposed essence of fire. They knew what it was, but they could not describe it with any precision. Many political and social science concepts suffer from the same problem. All good political scientists, for example, know that sovereignty is the supreme authority over a territory and its inhabitants. But what is meant by supreme authority? How can it be recognized, and with whom does supreme authority lie? Like phlogiston, "sovereignty" seems to refer to the essence of something, but its precise nature—in spite of the seeming clarity of definition—is never spelled out. A theory can be no more precise than its concepts. Specifically, what is it? Does it have clear boundaries? Where does it start? Where does it stop? What does it include? If a definition is obtuse, it is generally the fault of the definer, not the reader. If a thing cannot be described with clarity, maybe it doesn't exist. *The more precise a concept's definition, the greater its utility in research and theory building.*

The requirement that conceptual definitions be precise is clearly related to the requirement that concepts be capable of operationalization. The less precise the conceptual defintion, the greater the gap is likely to be between the conceptual definition and the narrowly restricted operational definition. When reading the discussion of power in Chapter 2, for example, consider whether the operational definitions of power are measuring "power" or a narrower concept, subsumed under the general umbrella of "power." Because we have measured one aspect within the general concept of power, can we assume that we have measured or demonstrated the existence of the entire concept?

Generality

A fourth requirement for the evaluation of concepts in political research is that a concept's *level of generality be as narrow and as specific as possible.* The proposition that voting behavior is influenced by an individual's personality, for example, suggests that voting may be influenced by values, habits, emotion, perceptions, motives, needs, or any one of several other suggested components of the human personality. It would be considerably more useful for political theory building to examine the influence of each specific component of personality in voting behavior. How do values influence voting? How do emotions influence voting?

Context

Concepts should be applied in the context for which they were developed. If a concept has been developed by psychologists to describe individual behavior, it should not be assumed to describe the behavior of groups or nations, as well. It is quite plausible, for example, to speak of the impact of an individual's personality on his political behavior. Yet because individuals possess personalities or "characters," it cannot automatically be assumed that groups and nations also have personalities or characters. One should not suppose that groups posses the same attributes as individuals until the proposition has been adequately demonstrated by empirical research, and vice versa.

Cultural Relativity

All concepts are not universal in their applicability. Many are indeed universally applicable, but this characteristic cannot be assumed. In cross-cultural studies of achievement motivation, for example, David C. McClelland found that the achievement motives existed in great abundance in economically developed societies but hardly at all in societies that were economically underdeveloped (see Chapter 6).

Also, concepts change their meaning from culture to culture. Behavior defined as authoritarian in the United States would generally be considered normal in the Middle East. Alienation, as defined in the impersonal, "dehumanizing" environment of the modern industrial society, would seem to be largely inapplicable to individuals living in the rural areas of Africa and Asia. Certainly the operational indicators would have to be different. The applicability of a concept to any society is a matter of empirical investigation.

Historical Relativity

Just as the meaning and applicability of concepts may vary from culture to culture, the meaning and applicability of concepts also may vary within the same culture over time. Using again the example of achievement motivation, we note that McClelland and his associates have found that Americans are becoming less achievement oriented over time. Accordingly, it would be a severe mistake to assume that achievement motivation will play the same role in shaping the behavior of future generations of Americans as it has in the past. *Concepts should be assumed to be applicable only for the times and places for which they have been empirically validated.*

Discretion

Some disciplines are more rigorous in defining and empirically validating their concepts than others. The same is true of subfields within disciplines. Within the discipline of psychology, for example, the behaviorists have perhaps the most rigorous empirical standards of any social science discipline; the Freudian analysts, the least. Political science clearly does not rank high on the list. Before using a borrowed concept to explain political phenomena, the political scientist would do well to examine its track record. How well has it been tested? How is it used by its advocates? On what grounds has it been criticized? Are there competing concepts or conceptual frameworks to explain the same behavior? If so, what are the empirical merits of each? Mere popularity within a discipline does not attest to a concept's validity. As one of our psychologist friends commented somewhat disparagingly, "Political scientists always seem to pick up the concepts that psychology has just discarded."

Causality

A final point of caution relates to the problem of causal inference. Simply because one concept is found to correlate highly with another, it cannot be assumed that the first concept causes the second. Anticipating an example from Chapter 3, we can point out that it is widely recognized that voting correlates highly with social status. The higher the status, the higher the voting. But income and education also correlate highly with voting. Which is the causal or explanatory concept: social status, income, or education? The statistical problems of causal inference are complex, and causality should not be lightly assumed.

AN ORGANIZATIONAL NOTE

In introducing the concepts and hypotheses from the fields of sociology, anthropology, economics and psychology, that relate directly to the analysis of political phenomena, and in illustrating and critiquing their use by political scientists, our presentation is made as simple and clear as possible, consistent with the demands of accuracy. Psychology concepts, for example, are introduced as they appear in the psychology literature as well as in the manner in which they have come to be used by political scientists. This step is essential if one is to understand the relevance of the concepts in question and be able to cope with the confusion surrounding the nomenclature in current political science literature. Once defined, the concepts are related to their potential use in analyzing problems drawn from representative subfields of political science. This step is followed, where feasible, by critical evaluation of political research attempting to utilize these concepts.

A few words on the format of the book are in order. We

had intended to organize materials around the traditional sub-fields of the discipline: American institutions, constitutional law, public administration, comparative government, international relations, international law, and political thought. Under this format, all the concepts and hypotheses relevant to the study of American institutions would have appeared in one chapter, those relevant to comparative politics in another, and so forth down the line. It soon became obvious, however, that researchers in all the traditional subfields had developed a keen interest in "political behavior," and the ordering of our discussion on concepts along subfield lines would merely result in duplication and redundancy. For better or for worse, the behavioral focus of modern political science has reduced much of the utility of defining along institutional lines.

To minimize overlapping and duplication and to maximize clarity of presentation, conceptual materials are presented on a discipline basis (e.g., sociological concepts, anthropological concepts, economic concepts, psychological concepts). To reduce overlapping, concepts common to more than one discipline are discussed only in the chapter in which their use seems most relevant to political analysis.

In terms of format, Chapter 2 discusses concepts used so broadly throughout the social sciences that they no longer belong to any particular discipline. As we see in analyzing these concepts, their breadth of application has done little to enhance their clarity. Chapter 2 also contains a brief evaluation of the most traditional political science concepts.

Chapters 3, 4, 5, and 6 are devoted to the discussion of sociological, anthropological, economic, and psychological concepts, respectively.

It has been a practical impossibility to cover all concepts and hypotheses developed by related social science disciplines that might potentially be relevant to political analysis. However, we have tried to include most of the concepts currently used by political scientists as well as many others that seem to be potentially useful.

NOTES

[1] For light, easily readable introductions to the scientific method, see: R. A. Baker, *A Stress Analysis of a Strapless Evening Gown* (Englewood Cliffs, N.J.: Prentice-Hall, 1963); J. B. Conant, *Science and Common Sense* (New Haven, Conn.: Yale University Press, 1951); Edward M. Segal and Garvin C. McCain, *The Game of Science* (Belmont, Calif.: Brooks/Cole, 1969). For more penetrating analyses of the scientific method see: Ernest Nagel, *The Structure of Science* (New York: Harcourt Brace Jovanovich, 1961); Carl G. Hempel, *Fundamentals of Concept Formation in Empirical Science* (Chicago: University of Chicago Press, 1952); T. Kuhn, *The Structure of Scientific Revolutions* (Chicago: University of Chicago Press, 1962).

[2] Carl Hoveland, "Concept Formation," *Encyclopedia Britannica*, vol. 6, (Chicago: Benton, 1964), p. 254. Other definitions that differ somewhat from the one offered in the text can be found in Abraham Kaplan, *The Conduct of Inquiry*, (San Francisco, Calif.: Chandler, 1964), pp. 48–49; and Vernon Van Dyke, *Political Science: A Philosophical Analysis* (Stanford, Calif.: Stanford University Press, 1960), p. 62. Also see Howard H. Kendler and Tracy S. Kendler, "Concept Formation," in *The International Encyclopedia of Social Sciences*, 1968; Carl G. Hempel, *Philosophy of Natural Science* (Englewood Cliffs, N.J., Prentice-Hall, 1966, passim. Also, Ernest Nagel and Carl G. Hempel, *Science, Language, and Human Rights*, vol. I. (Philadelphia: Eastern Division, American Philosophical Association, University of Pennsylvania Press, 1952), pp. 65–84.

[3] John C. McKinney, *Constructive Typology and Social Theory* (New York: Appleton-Century-Crofts, 1966).

[4] Thomas Hobbes, *Leviathan, 1651* (Indianapolis, Ind.: Bobbs-Merrill, 1958), pp. 109–110.

[5] For an extended discussion of theories, see Kaplan, *The Conduct of Inquiry*, chap. VIII.

[6] Anthony Downs, *An Economic Theory of Democracy* (New York: Harper & Row 1957), pp. 296–297.

[7] For an extensive discussion of the role of models in political science, see Robert T. Golembiewski, William A. Welsh, and William J. Crotty, *A Methodological Primer for Political Scientists* (Skokie, Ill.: Rand McNally, 1964).

[8] William H. Riker and William Zavoina, "Rational Behavior in Politics: Evidence from a Three Person Game," *American Political Science Review*, vol. 64, no. 1 (March 1970).

[9] For a general discussion, see Vernon Van Dyke, *Political Science: A Philosophical Analysis*, p. 107.

[10] Golembiewski et al., *A Methodological Primer for Political Scientists*, p. 437.

[11] Ibid., chap. VIII.

2

General Social Science Concepts

This book relates major concepts of sociology, anthropology, economics, and psychology to political analysis. Certain concepts, however, are not clearly identified with any specific discipline and are better thought of as general social science concepts. Systems, power, and communications, which clearly fall within this category, have become major areas of research in most social science disciplines.

In this chapter we briefly survey and critique the concepts of systems, power, and communications. Since applications of these general concepts occur quite regularly in the political science literature, our discussion is limited to outlining major features and critiquing conceptual utilites.

SYSTEMS ANALYSIS

The study of general systems represents an attempt by scholars in several disciplines to give structure to their particular areas of study while at the same time providing the basis for an exchange of insights between disciplines. This effort has received major impetus from the work of the biologist, Ludwig van Bertlanffy and from the Society for General Systems Research. The Society publishes a yearly research report in which scholars from all interested disciplines apply the idea of a system to their own research areas.

A *system* is any specified set of interacting variables. When we look at a biological or mechanical system, for example, we can identify its component parts as well as the interactions or interconnections between these parts necessary for the successful performance of the whole. Similarly, elements of a social system can be identified as the people, individually and in groups, who are members of the "system."

The development of the systems concept in political

science is most fully illustrated in the work of David Easton. A discussion of the framework he established, therefore, should provide a clearer idea of what political scientists mean by the political system and how it can help us to increase our understanding of political phenomena.

The basic idea of the political system is not very complex.[1] Its major elements, as indicated in Figure 2.1, are authorities, supports, demands, and feedback.

All political systems include certain *authorities*, who are responsible for making decisions. Such authorities may be a single indivdual, such as a king or a dictator; an oligarchy or a military junta; a town meeting, in which the total community participates in the decision-making process; or one of the almost infinite variety of representative systems to be found in the world today.

In a national political system, *support* by its members is needed on at least three levels. Easton defines these as the political community, the regime, and the authorities.[2] *Support* for the *political community* refers generally to the sense of being a part of something: The idea of being French, or American, or Mexican thus involves a pride in the community and a positive commitment to self-inclusion in the political system. The *regime* refers to the set of structural arrangements by which it is decided who the authorities will be and how they will proceed to make decisions. The *authorities* are the individuals who occupy the legitimized roles for making decisions.[3] Presidents and mayors are examples of individuals occupying legitimized roles for making decisions. If support for the authorities and their policies fails, stress is built up in the system. This loss of support may carry over to loss of support for the regime unless a mechanism for replacing authorities is available. Unless pro-

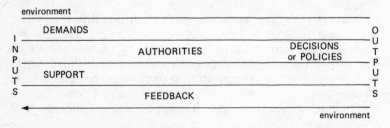

Figure 2.1

cedures for changing the rules of the regime can be established, loss of support at the regime level may lead to violent conflict and revolution. Regime change in the United States, for example, occurs as a result of constitutional amendment. Loss of support for the basic symbols of unity of the political community, needless to say, jeopardizes the existence of the entire system, including both the authorities and the regime.

SUPPORTS

Supports thus can be defined as any behavior that strengthens the position of authorities and the regime or increases the sense of community among members of the system. Such supports may be active, such as voting or serving in the armed forces, or they may be passive attitudes, such as "going along" and not causing trouble.

Demands are an important and distinct type of input into the political system. Directed at the authorities, demands may be urgent requests for change of policy or even for the replacement of the authorities. It must be remembered that demands do *not* include *all* attitudes and are *not* identical with public opinion. For example, a large majority of the American people favored federal aid to education several years before demands were made on the authorities to implement this policy.[4] Thus public opinion does *not* constitute a demand *unless* and *until* it is *articulated, organized, and pressed on the government.*

Easton uses this discussion of demands and supports to focus on a crucial problem facing all political systems: How can the quantity of demands be restricted or regulated to avoid overloading the system? Clearly, if demands exceed the capacity of the authorities and the regime to deal with them effectively, the resulting discontent will lead to intensified demands and sharply reduced supports, thereby jeopardizing the system. It is in this context that Easton introduces the concept of gatekeepers: individuals or institutions whose function is to restrict and filter both the types and the quantity of the specific demands that reach the point of decision by authorities. Different systems have different gatekeeping processes. In some systems gatekeeping
done by restricting the range of individuals who m

mately make and endorse demands. Thus in ancient Athens only male adult citizens could participate in the policy-making process. Medieval monarchies accomplished this screening by listening only to the nobility. Eighteenth-century America barred participation by women, slaves, and those who did not hold property. In Communist governments, only party members may legitimately pose formal political demands. In a modern democratic system, by contrast, each citizen is to some extent his own gatekeeper. Even so, opportunities for successful conversions of wants into demands are still quite limited, and the number of citizens who actually engage in the conversion process is relatively restricted. In the conclusion to their classical empirical study of the civic cultures, Almond and Verba, point out that the system would be untenable if every individual tried to press on the government the volume of demands which each seems to feel he is capable of successfully pursuing.[5]

Political parties and interest groups also restrict and focus the volume of demand flow, making it possible for the authorities to investigate alternatives and still have time and resources available to respond to some of the demands. It is easier for the government to deal with labor unions, for instance, than to confront each worker individually. Unions and similar groups have the crucial function by crystallizing demands and presenting them to the authorities in manageable form. Easton suggests, nevertheless, that in a democratic system the potential for an overload of demands on the system is very great, unless cultural rules prevent certain kinds of issue from arising frequently in the form of demands.[6] It appears that a government, even one we consider to be a good one, is least stable when a great number of demands are placed on it—a condition that is most likely to occur when the smallest number of obstacles to popular participation are constructed. The degree of success obtained by the minority of people who try to influence government policy thus seems to be dependent on self-restraint by the majority, whether conscious or unconscious.

Feedback refers to the information received by the authorities concerning the polity's response to their policies. An accurate appraisal of the feedback process is necessary both for the attainment of the goals of the authorities and for the maintenance of the regime. As discussed by Easton:

If a system is to be able to respond and thereby seek to cope with stress, what kind of information must it be able to obtain? It is clear that, first, the authorities in the system, those invested with the special responsibilities and powers to act in the name of the system, would need to know the conditions prevailing in the environment as well as in the system itself. In this way they could act so as to anticipate any circumstances that might lead to the withdrawal of support, whether diffuse or specific. Not only will the authorities frequently have a better opportunity to maintain the input of support if actions are taken before stress-provoking conditions occur; at times it is mandatory that such anticipatory measures be taken.

Second, the authorities must also seek to acquire information about the supportive state of mind of the members and the demands being voiced at least by the politically influential members of the system. It is important to know whether the members are acquiescent to the regime and solidary with the political community, or whether they are on the verge of revolt against both, and what their specific demands are.

Third, the authorities must obtain information about the effects which the outputs have already produced. But for this, the authorities would have to act in perpetual darkness. There must be a continuous flow of information back to them so that whatever their goals may be with respect to support or the fulfillment of demands, they are aware of the extent to which their prior or current outputs have succeeded in achieving these goals.[7]

Examining political phenomena in a systems perspective clearly aids the political scientists in visualizing key aspects of the political process. In particular, the concepts of supports, demands, and feedback emphasize the interdependence of leaders and citizens. Systems analysis also allows for an easy transfer of hypotheses from one level to another, through the identification of subsystems within a given political system. Thus we can think of the United States, France, and Japan as individual political systems and also, at the same time, as subsystems of the international political system. We can think of individual states in the United States as subsystems of the American political system. We can look at the member countries of the European Economic Community as individual political systems or at the EEC as a single political system, with the member countries as subsystems. For each political system, whether Florida or Missouri, Colombia or Germany, or the United Nations, we are directed to examine and describe changes in support and demand levels and in the effectiveness of policy output. Furthermore, systems analysis aids in pinpointing areas of weakness or potential danger in a political system. If the feedback process is found to be clogged, for example, it might be possible to predict that the authorities in that system were running a high risk of losing touch with their populations and might well embark on inappropriate policies.

Serious problems arise when we try to use the systems as a central framework for political analysis. Significantly, a systems analysis of a political system is valid only for the point in time at which it is made. Thus if weaknesses appear in the system, it is difficult to gauge their severity or to ascertain whether they are growing more or less severe without recourse to a series of systems analyses over several periods of time. This is not always feasible. Also, since the future performance of a political system may be radically altered by environmental factors, projections into the future can be tenuous at best. Moreover, because systems analysis is static, political systems often appear to be more stable or static than they actually are.[8] We elaborate on this point in the discussion of structural–functional analysis in Chapter 3.

Systems analysis also suffers from severe problems of operationalization. In the international system, for example, difficulties in identifying the authorities[9] have made it very hard to apply Easton's systems framework. Defining the boundaries of a given system does not seem difficult when the system is a modern industrialized state such as England, Germany, or the United States. But arriving at such a definition becomes more problematical when we deal with many of the developing areas. Is an individual who does not understand a nation's official language, or is unaware of the existence of the formal structure of government, a member of a given system just because he lives within the legal boundaries of that country? This situation is common among the more remote populations of many developing areas. Similarly, does the concept of authorities relate only to formal authorities, such as an executive or legislature, or to all individuals exerting influence on the decision-making process? If the latter is the case, the drawing of boundaries becomes truly difficult. The concepts of support and demands also are subject to considerable ambiguity. Is voting, for example, to be interpreted as a sign of acceptance of the political system or as a sign of alienation? In the first instance, it would be support; in the second, a demand. Following the same line of reasoning, failure to vote in the United States might well be a sign of systems support, whereas not voting in Italy might be an indication of distress. Such matters must be empirically resolved for each society studied, for each point in time.

In spite of these problems, systems analysis provides a basic framework that has been built on and elaborated by proponents of the structural–functional approach to societal analysis—an approach commonly used by and perhaps predominant among contemporary scholars in comparative, cross-national political analysis. Systems theory has also been heavily drawn on by those who see communications as a central focus for social analysis—an emphasis most articulately formulated in political science by Karl W. Deutsch.[10] Its most serious competitor as a central concept for political analysis is probably the concept of power, which deals with characteristics of individuals, groups, and nations, and relationships among them, rather than the internal structure and interrelatedness emphasized by a systems approach.

POWER

Power is considered by many political scientists to be the central organizing concept of the discipline. Perhaps the most visible advocate of this position is Hans J. Morgenthau. In *Politics Among Nations*, Morgenthau suggests that power is always the ultimate aim of politics, including international politics, and that everything not undertaken with this in mind is not and should not be considered to be political.[11]

Considerations of power seem to permeate political and social investigation. Although the concept has not been used consistently by all researchers, a certain level of agreement has been reached among its most systematic proponents concerning the nature and most appropriate use of power. Three common problems have been the source of most of the confusion. First, is power an absolute quantity? Is it something that can be held in measurable quantities by an individual, such as the President of the United States, or by a nation, such as the United States or the Soviet Union? Or, is it a relationship between individuals and groups which has distinctive meaning only when we focus on a particular issue or problem? Second, how do we measure power? Is it possible to come up with a unique operationalization, or must different kinds of power (political, economic, etc.) be measured differently? Third, is it necessary to distinguish between power and other similar concepts such as influence, authority, and leadership? And if so, how are such distinctions to be made?

Let us examine the first source of confusion. Is it more useful to consider power as a quantity or as a relationship? This very important distinction is best explained by analogy. In physics, we think of power as a measurable quantity that can be attributed to an individual human being, animal, or machine. In this context, power is defined as the capacity to move a given mass of resistance a given distance in a given time. Horsepower, for example, is a unit measure describing the power of engines in reference to the equivalent power of one or more horses. At least ideally, a 10-horsepower engine should possess sufficient power to move any object with a resistance of less than 10 horsepower.

Political scientists have found it virtually impossible to assign absolute power values to individuals or groups, appealing as the thought may seem.[12] We cannot speak of all 10-power individuals as having the power to move all 9-power individuals or of a 25-power President being able to move two 10-power congressmen. If and when political scientists acquire the capability of accurately measuring the resistance to change of all individuals whose attitudes or behavior are successfully altered by others, it might be possible to empirically measure political power as a quantity attributable to individuals or groups. Aside from gross estimates, we have yet to reach that point. Particularly problematic in this regard is the tendency of most political decisions and power relationships to involve the activities of several individuals and groups simultaneously. It is difficult if not impossible to isolate the effects of any one individual or group from the others, thereby to determine which individual or group is responsible for what quantities of the visible changes that are observed and measured by political scientists. For this reason, most investigators prefer to view political power as a relationship between individuals and groups rather than as a characteristic of individuals or groups.

We turn now to the second source of confusion. If power is considered to be a relationship rather than an attribute of individuals or groups, what factors must be taken into account in its measurement? In this regard, the formulation of power suggested by Robert A. Dahl is particularly useful. First, it means that we attempt to measure power in a particular situation or with respect to a particular issue.[13] Thus we refrain from making statements about the power of one individual or group over other individuals or groups except with reference to one issue or a series of identifiable issues. We might speak, for instance, of the power of the President over Congress in the area of foreign policy. By this we mean the probability that the President could secure from Congress acquiescence to his views and initiatives when only acquiescence was necessary and that he could mobilize popular support for his policies if this were also required. We could not, however, talk about the total power of the President except as we referred to some combination of his power as determined individually in a variety of issue areas and with respect to a variety of groups.

Dahl also suggests that in relationships among human actors, acquiescence is ordinarily involved on both sides. Thus power is viewed as a reciprocal relationship in which pay-offs go to the weaker party as well as to the stronger. If a government tries to mobilize the population in support of a policy, for example, it generally provides a series of inducements, if only symbolic, designed to gain popular support. Similarly, the President's exercise of power over Congress generally involves pay-offs for particular congressmen in terms of support for their programs or assistance for their constituents. Alfred Kuhn, in articulating this view of power, suggests that any such relationship is a transaction between the person attempting to exert power and the individual who is the object of these efforts.[14] Sorting out what reciprocal pay-offs might be included in each case, it should be noted, poses an analytical and empirical problem of formidable magnitude.

Jack H. Nagel suggests that a series of additional considerations is also involved in the attempt to use the concept of power in political research.[15] According to Nagel, we must be sensitive to:

a. The domain of power—over how many individuals does a given person exert power?
b. The range or scope of power—on how many issues or for which set of responses will each of these individuals be induced to change his positions and responses?
c. The basis of power—the ability and capacity to respond to and to satisfy the motives of those being induced to change.
d. The strength of power—how much can the position of others be effectively changed? Related to this is item e.
e. The amount and direction of power—will this change be sufficient to affect the others' positions at the point of decision?
f. The means of power—what various alternative methods are available for obtaining compliance?
g. The costs of exercising power—what other opportunities are given up, what chances for success in the future must be sacrificed, to obtain compliance of others in the present?

Simply stated, political power is very difficult to compare or even to discuss without specifying who is exerting power over whom, the issues at stake, and the techniques being used. Only when each of these aspects can be compared for a variety of situations can we hope to arrive at a single general measure for power.

In an attempt to overcome many of these problems, Dahl has produced a conceptual definition of power in algebraic language.[16] The formula is as follows:

$$(2.1) \qquad M_{Y/X,(a,b)} = \mathrm{Pr}\,(X, a \cdot Y, b) - \mathrm{Pr}\,(X, z \cdot Y, \overline{b})$$

This "language" actually is clearer and more concise than ordinary language, once the meanings of the terms are given. Here $M_{Y/X}$ refers to the power of the individual Y over individual X, where a is the issue being considered and b the specific technique or intiative being used by individual Y. The right side of the equation represents the probability that individual X will take the action desired by Y following Y's initiative b, minus the probability of X's taking the desired action in the absence of that initiative. This definition focuses on the particular behavior desired by one actor from the other, and the specific technique used to achieve this compliance. Political power for that individual with respect to a given relationship, based on the use of a given technique to achieve a particular goal, is defined as the probability of the desired action being taken in the presence of the use of the given technique minus the probability that that action would have occurred if the specific attempt to induce compliance had not been made.

This conceptual definition of power is applicable to a wide variety of political problems. We can, for example, pose the question of presidential power through investigating differences in the voting patterns of legislators on similar issues when the President does or does not attempt to utilize certain techniques for obtaining compliance. Thus if a certain number of legislators changed position on arms limitations as a result of a presidential address, we might use this as a measure of the Chief Executive's power.

Although our definition of power indicates some of the problems that must be considered, it is in need of improvement on conceptual and operational grounds. This way of looking at political power does not solve the problems associated with the empirical measurement of power. Some of the data needed may be unobtainable. Suppose we want to determine the power of United States Senators with respect to their colleagues on issues such as civil rights or advice and consent on presidential nominations. Needed data relating to the techniques and initiatives used by each senator to support or defeat a given action may not be recorded anywhere, however, which of course means that they will not be available to the researcher. If we are satisfied with a conceptual definition, this limitation would not be critical, since we would merely try to encourage senators to start recording such information for future study. The prospects for such cooperation, however, are less than encouraging.

Dahl's formula presents other problems as well. It is not useful, for example, in the investigation of cases in which the individual exerting power is attempting to prevent action or change by other individuals. Bachrach and Baratz suggest that this problem is particularly acute in attempts to analyze power structures of local communities.[17] This issue, often posed as a debate between elitists and pluralists, has stimulated considerable discussion concerning the use of power in the analysis of political problems.[18] Criticism of the elitist position—according to which a small minority control the major decisions in American communities—has been based on the following arguments:

a. If you start by asking "Who runs this community?" you have begged the important question of whether there is any elite that actually "runs the community." It may be, for example, that no one identifiable group runs things, and this possibility must not be excluded by the a priori assumption of research.
b. Elitists, it is suggested, presuppose the stability of the power elite. That is, they assume that the same minority is likely to continue to make the decisions for a considerable period of time, rather than doing careful investigations over time to see whether this assumption is correct.
c. Elitists are accused of equating reputed power and actual power. This is essentially a problem in conceptual definition. Of course the supposition by some that people get their own way in everything does not necessarily mean that they always do. However, if someone believes that you can achieve a given goal, he may be more likely to cooperate with you in achieving it. Although actual power and reputed power are not the same thing, they are related. We may not observe a particular individual or group taking any initiatives to change policy, but everyone may be aware that certain kinds of initiatives would be taken if they were necessary to prevent certain kinds of change. In conceptually defining power, therefore, we want to be aware of this possibility and allow for its inclusion.

This leads us to the consideration of two other important conceptual problems. First, is some action, initiative, or communication of preferences a necessary precondition for a power attempt? Nagel defines power in terms of the perceptions of the individual whose behavior is being changed, and he suggests that one actor has power over another if the second believes that retribution might be taken if he does not act.[19] This formulation, however, fails to acknowledge the possibility that these perceptions may be incorrect and may lead to actions that do not contribute to the achievement of anyone's actual goals. The situation is worth investigating, but is it power?

Second, must an individual's behavior change for us to say that someone has power over him? If one person convinces a majority in his community to oppose free trade with the Soviet Union, but they do nothing about it, can we meaningfully say that he has power over the others? Or might we call this influence, but not power?

This brings us to the third general area of confusion relating to the concept of power—that of distinguishing power from similar concepts. Defining power as a relationship puts it in the same category with concepts involving other such relationships and transactions. These include the concepts of conflict, bargaining, cooperation, rivalry, tension, and competition, as well as authority, influence, leadership, and control. Of particular concern are three closely related concepts—influence, leadership, and authority—and their relationship to power.

How indeed do we draw such distinctions? Perhaps we think of political influence as being more subtle than political power, authority as being more legitimate or making power easier to accept, and leadership as involving more personal qualities. But how do we carefully delineate these differences to make them useful in an empirically related research project? Many scholars, such as Cartwright, Dahl, and Nagel, do not bother to distinguish between power and influence.[20]

In the interests of conceptual clarity, we next suggest possible ways of drawing such distinctions.

Power and Influence

a. Power and influence are the same thing—namely, a change in attitudes and/or behavior of one actor as a result of his interaction with another actor. The difference is that power represents more of the same (i.e., a change of greater magnitude). In the words of Lasswell and Kaplan, power differs from influence in that the former involves "severe deprivation."[21]

b. Influence is power when exercised by those not having authority.[22]

c. Power is exerted whenever a change in behavior in a desired direction is induced by one actor in another, whereas for influence to be present such a change must also include modification in attitudes resulting in an agreement in goals between the two actors.

Power and Authority

Authority generally refers to the occupancy of a formal leadership role, such as the Presidency, which is accepted as legitimate by other actors in a given situation. Thus if someone has authority, it is considered proper for him to suggest appropriate behavior to others with respect to certain questions, and others will expect to comply with these suggestions. Authority is a contributor to the power of an individual in those areas in which his role is considered to be legitimate. It is therefore distinct from power, although individuals with higher degrees of authority usually have a greater amount of political power as well. As Richard Neustadt's 1960 work *Presidential Power* clearly indicates, however, the mere holding of authoritative office is not a guarantee of power. All American presidents clearly have not possessed equal power.

Power and Leadership

Leadership involves taking initiatives, suggesting courses of action to which others may react positively or negatively. Leadership includes that subset of power which consists of direct appeals to individuals to support a given course of action. It is a subset of the potential tactics available to an individual attempting to exercise power. Leadership may be successful or unsuccessful, but success in one case may be likely to increase the probability of success in another case.

We can look at leadership and influence as distinct subsets of power. Leadership refers to appeals to several actors at once, whereas influence refers to appeals to individual actors who probably hold key positions. Authority—a resource available to an individual attempting to exercise power—stems from the formal office or other high-status position he holds and can be classed along with such other resources as finances and personality characteristics.

The distinction between power and influence might be drawn in other ways. But these terms require that some such distinction be made and articulated. Whatever distinction is made, it will have implications for the meaningfulness of certain common statements. Suppose, for example, that influence and power are considered to be synonymous, with power merely representing more of the same. The common statement, "The more influence a man has, the more power he has," then becomes a definitional statement and cannot help solve any important practical problems.

What can we say about power as a central focusing concept for political research? First, it is intuitively appealing. Power seems to be a relevant factor in nearly every "political" situation or relationship. However, success in consistently operationalizing the concept has not been great. In fact, the debate in the conceptual definition of power is not over, and opinion on the relationship between power and other similar concepts remains divided. Too often the practice has been to use the same term in a variety of ways, conveniently fitting it to the argument of the moment. As a result, power is usually defined at least slightly differently in each separate research effort, greatly limiting the potential for precise comparison of findings and for the use of power as a central focusing concept.[23] Or, alternatively, it may be used so broadly that it means virtually anything. Nevertheless, there is a general agreement about its use by careful scholars in the field, and considerable agreement exists on the major problems to be overcome in making power an extremely useful focus for dealing with major political problems.

In summary, power does not rate particularly high in definitional exclusiveness. It is used to refer to a wide variety of relationships. Careful scholars such as Robert A. Dahl have made notable progress in sharpening the concept, but many scholars still use power in an imprecise way.

Power is also a very general concept, and some of the problems of conceptual clarity, particularly those of operationalization, are related to this generality. It will probably be necessary to focus on specific types of power, and alternative operational definitions of each, to reach a satisfactory solution of this problem.

COMMUNICATIONS

Systems theory covers the broad perspective of politics. Power focuses on paired relationships. Some scholars have felt that both perspectives could be combined by concentrating on the exchange of messages and the process of communication.

Communications are a basic element of any human society.

The complexity of human communication has been viewed as one of the most distinctive features of human organization. Communication has always been important, but recent expansion of the mass media has greatly increased our awareness of its significance. At the same time, the rapid growth of computer technology has led to careful investigation and analysis of information exchange and the processes by which it occurs.

Communications are the lifeblood of the political system. Without communications, such a system can neither establish nor maintain unity or interdependency. Without the preservation and transmission of records of what has been done in the past, the system lacks continuity.

In studying communications, we deal with several types of linkages. Of particular importance is the communication of content over space and over time. Communications over space involve both horizontal and vertical dimensions—that is, exchanges among decision makers, and between them and the rest of the population. Exchanges between decision makers and the public include television addresses by the President, letters to congressmen, campaign speeches, and votes in popular elections. They also include public protests and the response of government to such demonstrations. Exchanges among decision makers include debates over legislation, treaties, and presidential appointments, memoranda from one government office to another, and testimony by government officials at congressional subcommittee hearings. More personal exchanges of information among decision-making elites as well as among members of the public at large are included in the horizontal dimension.

Whereas communications over space focus on the contemporary political process, the analysis of communications over time leads us into the area of the transfer of records and norms from one generation to the next. This includes the transfer of ways of approaching politically relevant action in the community, thus the whole process of political socialization and its content political culture. The same kinds of issues are involved in the study of any entry into the political system. Whether the entrant is a young child or a newly arrived immigrant, the communication to him of his responsibilities and of the opportunities present within the system is essential if the system is to operate efficiently.

(See Chapters 4 and 6 for a further discussion of socialization and culture and their relevance to politics.) Perhaps the most complete attempt to use communication as a central focus for political analysis is the work of Karl W. Deutsch. Our discussion of the basic outlines of this approach leans heavily on his formulations in *Nerves of Government*.[24]

Since communications is the process of information exchange, we must deal with the concept of information. Essentially, information involves a patterning of communication. A crying baby, a barking dog, a tooting foghorn are communicating; but the amount of information is not very rich, although it may be adequate in some cases. Communication is much more efficient when we can sharpen and specify its content. When this is done, the responses of others to our efforts will no longer be in proportion to the amount of energy we put into our cry, but will be much more affected by our tone of voice and by the verbal content of the message. This is the difference between *power* engineering and *communication* engineering. Power produces changes; communication, on the other hand, triggers changes in a suitable receiver.[25]

The communications process triggers change through the exchange or transfer of information. Information can be thought of as patterned distribution or a patterned relationship among events.[26] The symbols and letters that make up the preceding sentence, for example, are patterned to form words, and the words themselves are arranged to carry an intelligible message. Thus the sentence contains information. The communication of information involves the preservation of patterns originating with the sender. Different channels of communications have different degrees of efficiency in preserving these characteristics. Thus a television broadcast carries more of the visual imagery of a football game than does a radio broadcast. And a modern stereo recording of a symphony carries more of the overtones in the music than does a monaural recording.

If a message is to be successfully communicated, at least some parts of the receiving system must be in a highly unstable equilibrium, to allow a relatively small amount of energy to successfully trigger a larger process of change. In an attempt to organize a protest, for example, the communication of a call to action will be less effective for individuals (receivers) who are not particularly dissatisfied with existing arrangements although the same content of communication is directed to all.

Thus in dealing with the role of ideas in prompting political reforms or inducing technological innovations, we are searching for potential instabilities among individuals in the communities in which such modifications are to be sought. Looking at the same problem from the point of view of the recipients of information, we focus on the selectivity of receivers—that is, the kinds of information accepted or rejected by them, based on the kind and amount of information they already have stored. Thus we may ask how many people, and which individuals are dissatisfied enough with perceived existing conditions and future trends to support changes of a given type. A lock can be opened either by a master key or by a key specifically fitted for that device. Similarly, individuals in a political system might be carried along with the crowd by a master orator but can be most effectively mobilized in a given direction by information directly adapted to their life circumstances and experiences. If we want people to support economic development, we need to find a way of suggesting minor changes that are reasonably sure to have an observable effect. If we want to get people to oppose war, or a particular war, we must make appeals that are relevant to and understood by our audience.

Information can be lost either through distortion or through failure to reproduce detail. Newspaper photos, for example, are not perfect reproductions of the information contained in the scene photographed. In listening to the voice of a friend over the telephone, we are well aware of the imperfect quality of the voice, due to the loss of overtones in the sound pattern. This too is a loss of information.

Information may be lost or distorted not only for technological reasons but also when messages are transferred from one individual to another through a series of intermediaries. In fact, a message carried person to person is not likely to retain much of its original content by the time it reaches the twentieth person.[27] There are four major points in the communication process at which distortion can set in. Problems exist at the source of the message, in the channels through which a message is carried, with the receiver, and in the feedback process.

A message sent by an individual involves a response to his own environment, and faulty or biased screening of environmental stimuli by the sender may result in information loss, producing distortion of the message. If the sender is distracted while sending the message, errors may occur in the encoding process (e.g., he may make a typing error or an incorrect data punch on a computer input card). These distortions may not make the message unreadable; but if compounded, they could result in a serious loss of information. Finally, poor judgment in the selection of channels through which a message is to be carried may lead to problems. The channel must be chosen to fit most appropriately the content of the message. In communicating detailed information about international trade or voting statistics, written records may be most appropriate. If the principal component of a message is its emotional content— an appeal to national unity or religious values—a personal verbal communication may preserve more of its essence.

The noise potential in the channel carrying the message is a second possible source of distortion. A distant radio station with lots of static can give us only incomplete and somewhat distorted information. A presidential address that is reported in the newspaper may suffer loss of information because only selected parts of the speech are printed or because of biased commentary on the editorial page.

Third, the message may be distorted by the receiver through inadequate monitoring, such as reading the sports page of the newspaper while an address is being presented on television. The receiver may also misinterpret the message, encouraged, perhaps by the transmission of a purposely ambiguous message. Or, the receiver may not know enough about the sender to properly interpret the message. The message may also be distorted through over- or under-emphasis on certain parts of a message because of crude volume and tone control in the message reproduction. An example would be the failure of the U.S. Department of State to hear the warning delivered from Moscow by George F. Kennan during the 1930s about the nature and intentions of the Soviet government.[28]

Finally, distortion may occur in the feedback process. The reactions of the message receiver may be misinterpreted by the sender, causing him to act inappropriately. Such problems seems to have caused difficulty for negotiators attempting to deescalate the conflict in Vietnam.

These kinds of distortion are potentially present in any exchange or transfer of information, and a way of measuring these distortions or the information loss produced by them is necessary in our attempt to apply communications ideas to social and political phenomena. The potential for such an application of information flows can be seen in the possibility of investigating the cohesion of organizations or groups of various types on the basis of their ability to transfer information among members with more or less delay and with more or less loss or distortion in the transmission. Thus we could say that a labor union is better organized than an agricultural organization if support of a strike or support of leaders for a political candidate is correctly communicated by the union to a certain percentage of the membership in a shorter time span. Carrying this one step further, we might be able to view an ethnic or cultural community, or even an entire political system, as a network of communication channels or chains of command; next we could measure the "integration" of individuals into that system by their ability to receive and transmit political information with little delay or loss of relevant detail. We could then regard power with respect to internal goals as the simultaneous presence within such a community of shared beliefs and efficient channels of social communication,[29] thereby gathering important data concerning the potential for cohesive action in the group or community.

Thus far we have discussed communications flowing from the sender to the receiver. The reverse flow of information—consisting of responses to the original message, or feedback—is also an important element of the communication process. Specifically, the clearer the feedback received by the message sender, the better able he is to make the adjustments necessary to the achievement of his goal.

Success in any communication process generally depends on four elements: load, lag, gain, and lead.[30] _Load_ refers to the extent or quantity of information that must be considered, as well as to the speed of changes in information needed for the system to respond to new information inputs. _Gain_ involves the size of steps that can be taken to respond to a given situation or goal. These steps may not be continuous; that is, the smallest possible corrective response may be greater than the amount of adjustment actually needed. Or it may be that precise changes require more time than is available before some corrective step is taken. A high rate of gain increases the probability of overcompensation. *Lead* refers to the distance of the predicted position of a moving target from the position from which the most recent signals were received.

In political terms, load refers to demands on the system and its authorities, whether international or domestic. *Lag* is a function of the speed and flexibility of decision makers and the decision-making structure in responding to such demands, including the efficiency of bureaucratic communication and control. Gain reflects the speed and intensity with which bureaucracies, interest groups, political organizations, and citizens respond to new information inputs with major recommitments of resources. For example, gain after Pearl Harbor was quite high. It was not difficult to mobilize the American people to intense support for war against Japan. The gain is also quite high in the case of some contemporary university administrators' responses on many campuses to student protest demonstrations. *Lead* involves the capability of authorities to predict and anticipate new problems effectively and to accurately gauge how rapidly the responses to established ways of doing things are changing in the views of the various constituencies.

Students of political development have found communications to be useful for studying both the response of authorities to changing circumstances and the outward spread of information discussed above.[31] Investigations of political development quite naturally involve study of the efficiency of governmental administration and communication, as well as increases in capabilities obtained through the successful spread of contemporary technology and skills and the orientations favorable in their application. The mass media of communication, travel, and the face-to-face spread of such information are recognized as important aspects of change in political systems and of development of more complex and flexible systems with greater all-around capabilities.[32]

Communications also provides an alternate model for those in new nations who believe that the effort to keep pace with existing demands must include a forced march toward modernization. Here a shift from *driving* to steering as the appropriate analogy for leadership is suggested for such systems.

The usefulness of a communications approach in the study of many problems is undeniable. A focus on the content and channels of communication is an important element, for example, in studies of political socialization, in investigations of the impact of the mass media, and in analysis of chains of command and the introduction and dissemination of rules in bureaucratic organizations.[33] Content analysis as a formal technique for testing hypotheses about the impact of communications has been intriguingly applied by David C. McClelland in studying the impact of mass media on popular attitudes.[34] And investigations such as those of Deutsch and associates show the application and use of communication flows in European countries and in the study of the process of political integration and cooperation in Europe.[35] In addition, the analysis of communication input provides a framework for the investigation of rational decision-making models, as well as other transactions among individuals and groups, such as cooperation and conflict.[36] The idea of deterrence, for example, assumes a focus on the communication process. The attempts to maintain a stockpile of weapons capable of destroying the adversary even after a first strike boils down to the efforts to communicate to the adversary a message that will make him believe this to be the case. As was pointed out in the movie *Dr. Strangelove*, a Doomsday machine defeats its own purpose *if you don't tell the other nations that you have it.*

In spite of the intuitive appeal of a communications approach to the study of political problems, its affinity with systems theory, and the potential for relating information transfer to the concept of power, there remain some serious problems in the development of a general theory of politics based on a communications framework. First, it is often very difficult to determine what is significant communication and what is not. Communication of information can be written or verbal or based on visual imagery; or, it may be a complex combination of these. Given time for analysis, written and verbal messages can be analyzed comparatively if allowances are made for symbolic elements contained in the tone of voice and facial expressions accompanying the verbal expression. Nevertheless, it is extremely difficult to attach a precise measure to such elements. It is also quite difficult to clearly define or measure message distortion. Attempts to do so are underway but are not yet generally applicable for research in political science.[37]

In addition, the basic data necessary for analysis of such communications received and exchanged by authorities may be extremely hard to obtain. Many important papers, including diplomatic and other decision-making documents, are likely to be classified, making them virtually inaccessible. Moreover, great technical expertise is required of the social scientist for fully successful application of the approach in such circumstances. A very high degree of language competency may also be essential. Yet another serious problem is the difficulty of measuring the correlations between what is said and what is done, when formal documents carry bluffs that may be understood by the recipient in a completely different fashion from that conveyed by the content of the message alone. The difference may be due as well to failure to recognize the important distinction between formal and informal communications.

In summary, communications is a concept of broad applicability in a variety of historical and cultural contexts. In terms of both precision and exclusiveness, communications is relatively clear, and specific kinds of communication can quite easily be defined for the purpose of hypothesis testing. Problems of operationalization remain the biggest handicap.

CRITIQUE

Critical evaluations, in the form of a general critique, are gathered at the end of each chapter that follows. Since this chapter is devoted to an overall assessment of these relatively distinct concepts, however, it seemed more logical to include the related critical evaluations within the general discussion.

NOTES

[1] David Easton, "An Approach to the Analysis of Political Systems," *World Politics* (1957), p. 384.

[2] David Easton, *A Systems Analysis of Political Life* (New York: Wiley, 1965).

[3] Legitimacy here refers to the acceptance by the relevant community of the way in which choices or decisions are made in that community. Legitimized roles are those which are so sanctioned by the community. Seymour Martin Lipset discusses the interaction between legitimacy and governmental effectiveness in *Political Man* (Garden City, N.Y.: Doubleday, 1960). See also chap. 3 in this book for a further discussion of roles.

[4] V. O. Key, *Public Opinion and American Democracy* (New York: A. Knopf, 1961), pp. 75, 88.

[5] Gabriel A. Almond and Sydney Verba, *The Civic Culture: Political Attitudes and Democracy in Five Nations* (Princeton, N.J.: Princeton University Press, 1963), especially chap. 15.

[6] David Easton, *A Systems Analysis of Political Life*, p. 99. We must, of course, specify the level of generality at which we are working, to be sure that our objectives and analysis remain clear and understandable.

[7] David Easton, *A Framework for Political Analysis* (Englewood Cliffs, N.J.: Prentice-Hall, 1965), pp. 128, 129.

[8] See the book review of David Easton, *A Systems Analysis of Political Life*, by Phillip Converse, *American Political Science Review* (December 1965), p. 1001.

[9] M. B. Nicholson and P. A. Reynolds, "General Systems, the International System, and the Eastonian Analysis," *Political Studies* (1969), pp. 12–31. Also see John W. Sutherland, *A General Systems Philosophy for the Social and Behavioral Sciences* (New York: Braziller, 1973). Also see Ervin Laszlo, ed., *The World System: Models, Norms, Applications* (New York: Braziller, 1973).

[10] Karl W. Deutsch, *The Nerves of Government: Models of Political Communication and Control* (New York: Free Press, 1966). See our discussion later in this chapter of the use of this concept.

[11] Hans J. Morgenthau, *Politics Among Nations: The Struggle for Power and Peace*, 3rd ed. (New York: Knopf, 1963), pp. 25–35.

[12] For a discussion of this and other related problems, see *Robert A. Dahl, Modern Political Analysis* (Englewood Cliffs, N.J.: Prentice-Hall, 1963).

[13] This is the thrust of Dahl's argument in "The Concept of Power," *Behavioral Science*, vol. 2 (July 1957).

[14] Alfred Kuhn, *A Study of Society: A Unified Approach* (Homewood, Ill.: Irwin, 1963), pp. 129–137.

[15] Jack H. Nagel, "Some Questions About the Concept of Power," *Behavioral Science*, vol. 13 (1968), pp. 129–137.

[16] Dahl, "The Concept of Power."

[17] Peter Bachrach and M. S. Baratz, "Two Faces of Power," *American Political Science Review*, vol. 13 (1963), pp. 632–642.

[18] Floyd Hunter, *Community Power Structure: A Study of Decision Makers* (Chapel Hill: University of North Carolina Press, 1953), p. 297;

Robert A. Dahl, *Who Governs?* (New Haven, Conn.: Yale University Press, 1961).

[19] See Nagel, "Some Questions About the Concept of Power," pp. 129–137.

[20] Darwin Cartwright, ed., "A Field Theoretical Conception of Power," *Studies in Social Power* (Ann Arbor, Mich.: Institute for Group Dynamics, 1959), pp. 183–220; Dahl, "The Concept of Power"; see Nagel, "Some Questions About the Concept of Power," pp. 129–137.

[21] Harold Lasswell and Abraham Kaplan, *Power and Society: A Framework for Political Inquiry* (New Haven, Conn.: Yale University Press, 1950).

[22] Cyril Roseman, Charles G. Mayo, and F. B. Collinge, *Dimensions of Political Analysis: An Introduction to the Contemporary Study of Politics* (Englewood Cliffs, N.J.: Prentice-Hall, 1966).

[23] Inis L. Claude, Jr., *Power and International Relations* (New York: Random House, 1962), pp. 12–39.

[24] Deutsch, *The Nerves of Government.*

[25] Norman Weiner, as quoted in Deutsch, *The Nerves of Government*, p. 146.

[26] See article by Anatol Rapaport, in Sidney Ulmer, ed. *Introductory Readings on Political Behavior* (Skokie, Ill.: Rand McNally, 1961).

[27] See Gordon W. Allport and Leo Postman, *The Psychology of Rumor* (New York: Holt, Rinehart & Winston, 1947).

[28] See Roseman et al., eds., *Dimensions of Political Analysis.*

[29] Deutsch, *The Nerves of Government*, pp. 110–127.

[30] Ibid., pp. 187–191.

[31] Lucian Pye, *Communications and Political Development* (Princeton, N.J.: Princeton University Press, 1963). See especially chaps 1, 4, 14, 17, and 18.

[32] Daniel Lerner, *The Passing of Traditional Society: Modernizing the Middle East* (New York: Free Press, 1956).

[33] Fred I. Greenstein, "The Benevolent Leader: Children's Images of Political Authority," *American Political Science Review*, vol. 54 (December 1960).

[34] David C. McClelland, *The Achieving Society* (New York: Van Nostrand Reinhold, 1961).

[35] Karl W. Deutsch and Richard Savage, "A Statistical Model of the Cross Analysis of Transaction Flows," *Econometrika*, vol. 28, no. 3 (July 1960), pp. 551–572.

[36] Rudolph Rummell has done a lot of work in this area, especially in articles appearing in the *Yearbook for the Society for General Systems Research*, and the *Journal of Conflict Resolution.*

[37] See Anatol Rapaport, in Sidney Ulmer, ed., *Introductory Readings on Political Behavior.*

3

Some Concepts of Sociology

More than any other social science discipline, sociology attempts to define the structures that give form to human society and to analyze the influence of such structures on human behavior. As political scientists have come to view political institutions and processes as social entities rather than legal artifacts, it is only natural for them to begin to rely heavily on the concepts and conceptual frameworks of their sociological colleagues. Indeed, one sociologist, perhaps in jest, has implied that political science might well be considered to be a subfield of sociology.[1]

For the sake of clarity, the ensuing discussion of sociological concepts is divided into two parts: concepts related to social structures, and concepts related to functions performed by social structures. The discussion of structure and function is followed by a critique of sociological concepts. The concept of culture, generally associated with sociology, is discussed in Chapter 4 in the context of political culture.

SOCIAL STRUCTURE

A social structure, in the broadest sense, is an established pattern of human interaction.[2] This general definition comprises informal groups that may persist for brief periods, and elaborate social systems that may endure for centuries. From the perspective of the political scientists, the crucial element common to formal and informal social structures is that they *do* influence political behavior. Within this context, the present chapter considers the political relevance of such social structures as roles, groups, small groups, and social class.

ROLE

All the world's a stage
And all the men and women merely players:
They have their exits and their entrances;
And one man in his time plays many parts,
His acts being seven ages. At first the infant,
Mewling and puking in the nurse's arms. . . .[3]

The concept of role in social analysis is directly analogous to the concept of role in theater. Just as the actors play specific parts or occupy specific positions on the stage, individuals occupy specific positions and roles in life.[4]

Roles are the basic units or building blocks of social structure; all other social structures are more or less complex networks of interrelated roles. A typical nuclear family, for example, is constructed of the roles of mother, father, child, and grandparents. Although society was earlier defined as the established pattern of human interactions, it could no less accurately be defined as established networks of interconnected roles.

Distinct but perhaps inseparable from the concept of the role is the concept of the *norm*.[5] *Norms* are the societal or cultural expectations defining how roles should be played. They provide the *content* of roles. The role of mother, for example, is universal to all family structures, regardless of variations in the complexity of the family structure, cultural values, or geographic location. Norms, by contrast, define the rights, duties, and relationships of the mother vis à vis other members of the family, and they differ radically from culture to culture.

The relationship of role to norm varies considerably according to different theorists, creating a certain amount of intellectual confusion. Some diverse meanings of the two concepts are summarized in Table 3.1, adapted from Biddle and Thomas's *Role Theory: Concepts and Research.*

Most political and social scientists use the concept role to include both position and norm. In discussing the role of judges in the role of senators, for example, political researchers usually mean both the structured position of judge as senator and societal expectations defining how judges and senators should play each role. The remainder of this discussion treats the concept of role as if it included the

Table 3.1

	Common-Language Meanings	Selected Meanings in Role Theory
Norm	(L, *norma*: a rule, pattern, or carpenter's square) 1. A rule or authoritative standard; a model, type, or pattern. 2. A standard of development of achievement; the mode or median.	1. A standard held for the behavior of a person or group. 2. A description of, or concept held about, a behavior pattern likely to be exhibited by a person or group. 3. Behavioral uniformity of actors. 4. Role.
Position (or Social Position)	1. A positioning or placing; the manner in which anything is placed. 2. An office, rank, status, or employment. 3. A spot, place, or condition giving one an advantage over another.	1. A designated location in the structure of a social system. 2. A set of persons sharing common attributes or treated similarly by others. 3. A role.
Role	(F: the role on which an actor's part is written) 1. A part or character performed by an actor in a drama. 2. A part or function taken or assumed by any person or structure.	1. A behavioral repertoire characteristic of a person or a position. 2. A set of standards, descriptions, norms, or concepts held (by anyone) for the behaviors of a person or a position. 3. A position.

Source: Bruce J. Biddle and Edwin J. Thomas, eds., *Role Theory: Concepts and Research* (New York: Wiley, 1966), pp. 11–12.

concept of norm. The distinction between the two concepts is important, however, and should not be lost sight of.

As an analytic tool, the concept of role gives promise of tremendous predictive ability for the social scientist. One might predict, for example, that the behavior of any man occupying the presidency of the United States, regardless of how extreme his campaign rhetoric, would be severely moderated by the structure of the role "President." Thus although the policies pursued by a President George Wallace would differ from the policies pursued by a President George McGovern, the differences would not reflect the great ideological differences apparent in the campaign rhetoric of each man. As a case in point, Lester Maddox, who used axe handles to enforce the racial segregation in his restaurant dramatically increased the number or black positions in the Georgia civil service in his role as governor. Why? Along similar lines, a substantial body of research including Ralph K. Huitt's "Democratic Party Leadership in the Senate" and Donald R. Matthews's "U.S. Senators and Their World" indicates that the behavior of senators is severely modified by pressure to conform to senate norms.[6] The same research also suggests that senators select specific roles for themselves and that their behavior is significantly influenced by efforts to conform to the demands of the assumed role. The fruitful application of role analysis in the U.S. Senate suggests that studies of this body might furnish good models for analyzing most legislatures.

Political scientists find role to be a useful analytical concept, but the original promise of role as an explanatory concept has not been fulfilled. One serious problem arises because each individual plays a multiplicity of roles. The position of President, for example, embodies several distinct roles, including chief of state, chief of political party, and chief domestic policy maker. The demands of the "chief of state" role impose the obligation of minimizing partisan considerations in making policy decisions. The role of "party chief," on the other hand, calls for the role incumbent to maximize party gain. Before the concept of role can predict behavior with any degree of precision, it must be ascertained which of the various roles the President or any political actor will play at any particular moment, and whether he will try to merge various roles, thereby producing yet another set of outcomes. Although the need to cope with the problems of role multiplicity and role conflict does not eliminate role analysis as a useful tool of political analysis, it clearly makes it a complex one.

A related problem is that individuals perceive role requirements in different terms. In using role concepts to analyze legislative behavior, for example, John C. Wahlke found the behavior of legislators to vary markedly depending on whether they perceived their role in terms of accurately expressing the opinion of their constituents or in terms of exercising their best judgment on the issues at hand.[7] Similarly, a host of personality variables to be discussed in

Chapter 6 clearly influence the way individuals perceive and interpret their roles and how effectively they execute their requirements.

GROUPS

Groups are among the most salient political structures in the United States, perhaps in the world. Starting with the publication of Arthur F. Bentley's *The Process of Government* in 1908, the concept of group has been a persistent if fluctuating focus of political analysis.[8]

A group consists of people who share a common characteristic. More than that, a group consists of people who share common goals and interact with each other concerning these goals. Thus young people or blondes or people with black skin form categories of people with a common characteristic. No category constitutes a group, however, until it has a shared goal, such as equal opportunity, equal rights, equal treatment, and until members interact with one another in relation to the achievement of this goal.[9] Youth, as a whole, do not make up a group. The Young Americans for Freedom and the Young Socialist Alliance do. The structure or boundary is provided by the interaction of a group's members.

The strength of a group is determined by several factors. Among the most important are: size of membership, financial resources, quality of leadership, organizational capacity, cohesion, group status, and the fit between the ideology of the group and the ideology of the community.

In terms of size, larger groups generally have more influence on legislators and other political officials than smaller groups. All things being equal, larger groups simply have more votes, more wealth, and greater quantities of other political resources.

Financial resources rival size in importance because of the flexibility they provide groups in financing the campaigns of desired candidates, in molding public opinion through extensive advertising campaigns (and thereby influencing politicians indirectly), and in maintaining extensive lobbying activities. Thus the numbers of large but poorly financed groups are often more than offset by the affluence of smaller groups.

Cohesion is important both to the effective action taken by

the group and to its credibility. If a legislator ignores a group's representatives, and 50 percent of the members still vote for him, he may well continue to ignore them. If 80 percent vote against him, he will probably listen the next time, unless of course 80 percent of the group's members had always voted against him. *Cohesion*, then, refers to the ability of the group to stick together and to their willingness to act on the basis of their shared goals.

The effectiveness of a group is also influenced by organizational strength. A group with a large, well-organized staff can more readily work to improve communication and cohesion within its ranks than a group lacking an organizational apparatus. It can also spend more time on lobbying, fund raising, and other essential support services.

The ideology and social status of the group also appear to contribute significantly to the potential influence of the group. Most legislators and other political officials, for example, are more likely to feel less negative pressure from their constituents for supporting ideologically pure and socially accepted groups, such as the Chamber of Commerce, than they would receive if they were to become identified with the John Birch Society or the Black Panther Party.

Collectively, the above-mentioned factors add up to what David B. Truman has referred to as *access*:

In the governmental activity of interest groups . . . power of any kind cannot be reached by a political interest group, or its leaders, without access to one or more key points of decision in the government. Access, therefore, becomes the facilitating intermediate objective of political interest groups. The development and improvement of such access is a common denominator of the tactics of all of them, frequently leading to efforts to exclude competing groups from equivalent access or to set up new decision points access to which can be monopolized by a particular group. Toward whatever institution of government we observe interest groups operating, the common feature of all their efforts is the attempt to achieve effective access to points of decision.[10]

The more favorably situated a group is in terms of size, financial position, leadership, organization, cohesion, ideology, and status, the greater its ability to dominate the access or decision points of government, and the greater its ability to achieve its goals.

Truman's concept of access is particularly interesting in that it permits an apparent distinction between the ability to gain access to the points of decision and the fact of actually exerting influence over the decision-making process. Although the process of gaining access and exerting influence are both affected by the variables just named, Truman seems to imply that access does not automatically lead to influence.

The effects of interest groups are felt at all levels of government: state and local, national, and international. A brief summary of three recent studies will help illustrate these effects.

At the state level, Lewis A. Froman, Jr., found that states with strong interest groups have long state constitutions and more constitutional amendments; they are also more likely to choose state agency chiefs, members of public utilities commissions, and state supreme court justices by popular elections, as opposed to having them appointed.[11] Interest group leaders found these arrangements to be favorable to them in obtaining advantages for their groups. A longer constitution means that only specialists can understand the law and its loopholes, and elections for judges and members of regulatory commissions give groups an opportunity to work for the election of persons sympathetic to their views in contests in which the public takes little interest.

Groups often try to form coalitions with other groups to more effectively attain their goals. A recent study by Robert L. Ross showed that in choosing coalition partners, groups tend to prefer ad hoc coalitions with other groups who share their interest on a given bill, though other groups who have advanced similar legislative objectives over a period of years are also viewed as desirable partners.[12] Personal friendship, or becoming involved in bills of little interest to your particular group, are not considered very important.

Groups prefer to fight battles where they have the greatest amount of strength. A locally concentrated group will generally favor seeing decisions made at the local level. A group with nationwide distribution will often prefer national decision making. This preference is illustrated by Robert J. Lieber's study of the attitudes of British interest groups toward British entry into the European Common Market.[13] Lieber shows a fairly consistent opposition to the surrender of British sovereignty to a larger unit. Even though many of the members (i.e., individual Britons) might be expected to benefit, the existing national groups would have less influence in the larger body.

Attempts to build a theory of politics around the concepts of group interaction and group conflict have generally found wide support among political scientists. Problems of operationalization and measurement, however, have thus far been insurmountable, and "group theory" remains a concept that has not advanced to the empirical level.[14]

The boundaries of most groups are fluctuating and imprecise, and this is a serious problem in studying groups. Is the influence of black organizations such as the NAACP based on the size of the group's card-carrying membership, or is it presumed to have a much larger informal membership that is not reflected in its organizational rolls? If it is presumed to be larger, how much larger, and who decides? Furthermore, if the informal membership is presumed to be larger, will it remain constant over a period of years, or will it fluctuate from issue to issue? Such difficulties might be overcome, but not without considerable effort.

In addition, just as individuals play more than one role, they generally belong to more than one group. Accordingly, the intensity with which a person will support any one group depends on such factors as the number and types of group, the intensity of one's commitment to each group, and the issues involved: If all his membership groups favor a particular issue, his support will be more intense than if his loyalties were divided.

Yet another difficulty relates to the difference between access and influence discussed earlier. Because certain groups appear to have access to decision points, can one assume that their access automatically resulted in influence? If so, was the fact of group access to the decision process the sole factor influencing the decision or one of several factors? Such questions are often difficult to answer in non-impressionistic terms.

Small Group

The attention of political scientists has been concentrated on formal interest groups of considerable size, but an interest in small groups is becoming increasingly apparent.

The essential characteristic of the *small group* is that its members interact with each other on a face-to-face basis with sufficient frequency to develop a personal awareness of each other. As defined by Robert F. Bales:

A small group is defined as any number of persons engaged in interaction with each other in a single face-to-face meeting or a series of such meetings, in which each member receives some impression or perception of each other member distinct enough so that he can, either at the time or in later questioning, give some reaction to each of the others as an individual person, even though it is only to recall that the other person was present.[15]

Small groups, then, may range from informal, two-person discussion groups through formal, structured groups such as United States Senate. Just how many people can meaningfully interact on a face-to-face basis is an open question.

The importance of the small group as a unit of social and political analysis rests on the well-documented proposition that each small group situation creates a social and psychological environment capable of modifying the behavior of its members. Office groups, for example, tend to evolve norms of proper dress, good conduct, and fair play. To gain acceptance and to avoid social ostracism, individuals joining the group are often willing to modify their own behavior to meet those norms. Similarly, small groups tend to evolve status hierarchies. Street gangs, for example, not only have norms of expected behavior but also evolve clear pecking orders defining the relative status and importance of each member. "Top dogs" not only play a greater role in determining the norms of the group, they enjoy greater latitude in violating them. Perhaps the best general reference for the dynamics of small groups and their ability to modify behavior is the recent edition of Cartwright and Zander's *Group Dynamics*.[16]

Small groups are ubiquitous in the political process. Courts, juries, regulatory agencies, legislative committees, and city councils are all small groups. So is the entourage of advisors that surrounds presidents, governors, and other executives. Clearly, the better political scientists can understand the dynamics of small group structure and interaction, the better able they will be to analyze the decision-making and leadership processes that occur in such groups.

Small group analysis would seem to be equally relevant to

the study of public administration, political socialization, and attitude change. In terms of public administration, most bureaucratic situations are small group situations. This is true of the office environment in which bureaucrats work and of their regularized interactions with the clients they serve, as well. Among other things, the norms and the psychological environment of the small group seem to be directly related to such factors as job satisfaction, level of output, bureaucratic innovation, and client satisfaction.

In terms of the acquisition and modification of political values, the role of small groups is equally vital. The family, the peer group, and the classroom are among the most important agents in the socialization process. It is within the limits of these groups that individuals acquire their basic attitudes, and it is through these and such other small groups as the local union, business club, and church group that basic attitudes are often reinforced or challenged.

Although much of the political process occurs in a small group context, the small group is important to political analysis for yet other reasons. Small groups offer the political scientist his best opportunity to engage in controlled experimental research. Because small groups are in fact small, experimenters can create controlled test situations in which diverse facets of processes such as decision making and opinion change can be individually manipulated and compared with the behavior of control groups. The results of such experimental studies cannot be presumed to perfectly replicate the real world, but they provide a fresh perspective for political research. At the very least, small group experiments furnish the basis for further examining and testing the findings of field research as well as for generating new hypotheses and guiding the efforts of field research.

One of the earliest and best known examples of experimental small group research in the political context is Ronald Lippitt and Ralph K. White's "An Experimental Study of Leadership and Group Life."[17] In this study children at a summer camp were divided into three groups for making crafts; the subjects were matched for I.Q., popularity, physical energy, and leadership. Leaders were assigned to the three groups and told to exhibit three different styles of leadership with the three different groups: authoritarian, democratic, and laissez-faire. The results showed that satisfaction with the work was greatest with the democratic group, whereas the democratic and authoritarian groups both accomplished more than did the laissez-faire group. Such results may not be directly applicable to large populations, but they might be applicable to the kinds of small governmental groups mentioned previously. More recent small groups experiments such as those conducted by James W. Dyson and his associates have focused on the impact of the small groups situation in facilitating political learning and opinion change.[18] An excellent survey of small group studies and their relevance to political analysis can be found in Sidney Verba's *Small Groups and Political Analysis*.[19]

Although experimental political research is yet in its initial stage, the small group format gives the political scientist a promising avenue for controlled experimentation —something he has heretofore lacked. Whether the rigorous format of controlled experiments will introduce greater precision into political conceptualizing, however, remains to be seen.

SOCIAL STRATIFICATION

Structures such as roles and groups may modify the individual's political behavior by (1) restricting his field of action and (2) influencing his attitudes, values, expectations, and general orientation toward politics. In addition to groups and organizations, however, societies are also segmented or stratified into a wide variety of social structures that may include family and lineage lines, class and caste lines, religious lines, ethnic (and racial) lines, and in many societies, even linguistic lines.[20]

The lines of stratification and their importance in shaping individual behavior, of course, vary markedly from country to country. In many of the less developed areas the most crucial lines of stratification are those of lineage (family, clan, and tribe). In the United States, the most salient lines of stratification are clearly racial and ethnic, followed at some distance by class divisions based largely on occupation and income. Stratification in the Soviet Union follows yet another pattern, with class lines apparently based on a complex blend of political power, intellectual attainment, and occupational status. As studied by Alex Inkeles, Soviet stratification lines take the following order:

1. Ruling elite
2. Superior intelligentsia
3. General intelligentsia
4. Working-class aristocracy (most highly skilled and productive workers)
5.5 White collar
5.5 Well-to-do peasants
7. Average workers
8. Average peasants
9. Disadvantaged workers?
10. Forced labor.[21]

The influence of social stratification on political behavior can be both varied and profound. In assessing the impact of economic class on voting patterns, for instance, Seymour Martin Lipset concludes that

More than anything else the party struggle is a conflict among classes, and the most impressive single fact about political party support is that in virtually every economically developed country the lower income groups vote mainly for parties of the left, while the higher income groups vote mainly for parties of the right.[22]

Marxist theorists, of course, have long cited the division of industrial societies into the capitalist class and proletariat classes as the primary cause of political conflict. Given the structural arrangements in which capitalists live, the argument runs, capitalists have no option but to oppress the masses, thereby forcing them into revolutionary action. Capitalists who do not oppress the workers cannot survive and will be cannibalized in the struggle for wealth and power. Marx's dire prophecy of class conflict has not been realized in the United States, but one of the major debates within American politics is whether, indeed, the United States is dominated by a narrow capitalistic elite. A full review of this debate exceeds the scope of this chapter. Its basic dimensions are outlined in the introduction to Thomas R. Dye and L. Harmon Ziegler's *The Few and the Many.*

Elitism asserts that society is divided among the few who have power and the many who do not. The powerful few are not typical of the masses in either background or attitude. They are drawn disproportionately from the upper socioeconomic strata of society and are in a position to control societal resources. These few also share a consensus which favors the interests of basic elites rather than demands of masses. Elitism proposes that changes in public policy are incremental rather than revolutionary, and that the movement of non-elites into elite positions is slow and limited only to non-elites who have accepted elite values. Finally, elitism argues that elites influence masses more than masses influence elites.

In contrast, pluralism is a belief that democratic values can be preserved in an urban, industrial, technological society by a system of multiple competing elites among whom power is fragmented and diffused. It asserts that non-elites can become elites by becoming active in public affairs and by acquiring information about issues, knowledge about democratic processes, and skill in leadership, organization, and public relations. Pluralism notes that voters can influence public policy by choosing between competing elites in elections, and that the party system allows effective policy choice. Masses also exercise influence over elites through membership in organizations which are active in public affairs and have sufficient power to hold elites accountable for their decisions. Pluralism defends the concept of competition among elites and the belief that different elites govern in different issue areas, hence no single elite can dominate decision-making in society.[23]

The pluralist position finds its roots in Truman's *The Governmental Process* and Dahl's *Who Governs?*[24] In different ways, both books illustrate how policy decisions have emerged as a result of conflict among competing elites and their supporters. Furthermore, both works suggest that conflict between elites forces the competing elites to enlist broad public support of their positions, thereby assuring public access to the decision-making process.

The elitist position finds its roots in Charles Beard's *An Economic Interpretation of the Constitution*, C. Wright Mills's *The Power Elite*, Willam Domhoff's *Who Rules America?*, and Floyd Hunter's *Community Power Structure*.[25] The elitist works suggest that a narrow capitalist elite plays a major role in *shaping* all policies that it considers to be important, regardless of the level of mass participation. Particularly significant is the proposition that elected political leaders are only secondary elites whose primary responsibility is to execute the behind-the-scenes decisions of the dominant capitalistic "power elite."

Because of the empirical problems involved in unraveling the mosaic of decision-making and elite–mass interactions, the debate is likely to remain unresolved for some time. Full understanding of the problem is also hindered because the pluralist–elitist conflict touches the raw ideological nerves of its practitioners. Most research seems to be more concerned with proving a point of view than with letting the empirical chips fall where they may.

The analysis of social stratification is equally crucial to the study of political integration or "nation building." Before leaders in the developing areas can weld their states into viable economic and political units, for example, ways must be found to penetrate and weaken the tribal, ethnic, and religious barriers that have been hardened by centuries of conflict. This is not to suggest that rigid stratification lines can or should be totally eliminated; some means, however, must be provided for linking and making the diverse strata of society responsive to the central government. This integration process, according to the Committee for Comparative Politics of the Social Science Research Council, calls for the reconciling of at least five steps or crises: identity, legitimacy, penetration, participation, and distribution.[26] *Identity* in this context means that identification with the state must be more intense than association with tribes, ethnic groups, religions, or other parochial strata. When identifications with the state are not dominant, the stability of the state is threatened with civil conflict every time a particular stratum is asked to make severe sacrifice for the good of the state.

Legitimacy refers to the requirement that individuals in all strata of society believe the governmental institutions of the state to be well suited to their needs. *Penetration* indicates the ability of the state to effectively reach all strata of the population in administering state policies. *Participation* similarly refers to the ability of governmental institutions to elicit *supportive* participation in political affairs from all strata of society. Finally, *distribution* refers to the need of all strata of society to share in the apportionment of a society's wealth and other values.

The five steps are clearly interrelated. The more individuals identify with the society or nation, the more likely they are to find established political institutions to be legitimate. The converse would also appear to be true. Similarly, the greater the ability of the central government to penetrate all strata of society, to elicit supportive participation, and to provide a satisfactory distribution of resources, the greater its ability to foster attitudes of identification and legitimacy by (1) socializing individuals to believe in the state and the nation and (2) demonstrating the utility of supporting the state through increasing the levels of goods and services available to its members. The Committee on Comparative Politics referred to the five steps as "crises" because of the extreme difficulty most developing areas experience in coping with the problems of stratification, the tragic conflicts in Biafra (Nigeria) and Bangla Desh (Pakistan) being cases in point.

It is also possible to view the international system or community from an international relations perspective—that is, as being stratified into nations and ideological blocs. If international integration is to be achieved at either the regional or the world level, the same problems of identity, legitimacy, penetration, participation, and distribution must be overcome.[27] Just as leaders of the developing areas are hard put to persuade members of their states to think in national rather than parochial terms, advocates of world governments encounter difficulty in inducing members of the world community to think in international rather than nationalistic terms.

Although social stratification clearly influences political behavior, the nature and extent of this influence is often difficult to ascertain precisely. It is particularly difficult to determine whether political behavior is influenced by the existence of stratification lines as such, or by one or more factors found within the strata. For example, middle-class Americans vote at a higher rate than lower-class Americans. Can we explain this behavior by the existence of social classes in the United States or by noting that members of the lower class are often less well educated and have less access to information? Which is the explanatory variable:

class, information, or education? The mere existence of stratification lines cannot presume political influence.

FUNCTION

Up to this point, the concepts surveyed have related to various forms of social structure. A second set of sociological concepts widely used by political scientists relates to the functions performed by social structures. As with so many other social science concepts, the diverse usage of the concept of function has severely reduced its clarity. Thus a university student might be exposed to the use of the term in a morning lecture in mathematics class. Later in the afternoon, he may encounter the term in an article by a sociologist or a social anthropologist, used with different referents and definitional implications. Even when we limit the use and definition of "function" within the discipline of political science, severe ambiguities remain.

To dispel some of the confusion that has attended the use of this concept and the approaches identified with, we rely on a three-way classification originally developed by William Flanagan and Edwin Fogelman.[28] These authors divide the use of function in social analysis into *eclectic functionalism, empirical functionalism*, and *structural functional analysis*.

The eclectic use of the concept is based on the premise that certain political structures can be viewed in terms of the functions that they perform, either individually or in combination with other structures, relevant to specific purposes. We can thus examine the Supreme Court of the United States in terms of the functions it performs with respect to the formation of public opinion, or in connection with the function it performs as a check on the President. Functions performed by the family in recently industrialized nations, or those performed by the military in developing areas, are also potential topics for investigation. When used in this fashion, the concept is extremely flexible in that it is merely one of many perspectives that might be profitably used to gain additional perspective for description and analysis. In this application of function, there is no attempt to assert the supremacy of any single concept as the basis for theory building. Thus it appears that function has been used, at least implicitly, by most political scientists who have written in the past, and virtually all the members of the discipline today.[29]

The *empirical* use of the concept of function is somewhat more rigid than the *eclectic* use. Here "function" includes not only the *intended* functions performed by a given political phenomenon but also the latent, or *unintended*, functions.[30] The *empirical* functionalist assumes that although functional emphasis is not *necessarily* the basis of a *general theory of politics*, it demands recognition as an avenue to the development of such theory. In short, the theoretical potential of the concept of function is more heavily emphasized by empirical functionalists than by the eclectic functionalist, and the application of the concept is both more clearly structured and broader in scope.

The classic application of *empirical* functionalism is the study by Robert K. Merton of the functions performed by the big city political "machines" and the bases of their support in the latter nineteenth and early twentieth centuries.[31] Merton examined the operations of the machines largely from the perspective of the functions they actually performed in the community. Of course, the *raison d'être* of the machines was the attainment and maintenance of political control, with all the accompanying patronage. According to Merton, this would be termed a *manifest* (or intended) *function*.[32] To accomplish this task, the machine had to marshal popular support, such as loyalty and, of course, votes. The machines used a variety of procedures to obtain support, including gifts of food and drink, arranging loans (and often bail), finding employment for constituents, and other similar services. In short, the machines frequently performed a kind of social welfare function prior to the development of more formal programs by the federal and local governments. Merton has labeled this type of function a *latent* (or essentially unintended) function.

Merton suggests that a given type of social organization, institution, or other type of social structure *may* perform both intended *and* unintended functions. Inefficient performance of intended functions might facilitate change, or indeed promote it. Latent functions may also have the result of promoting social change. In the context of this example, the social welfare functions performed by the machines may have prompted further demands for governmental welfare programs. In any event, once the latent functions of the machines were replaced by other political phenomena contributing to the performance of the same function, the machines lost most of the support they had garnered via their mobilization techniques. Thus, in a way, the discharge of latent functions represents a potential catalyst for social change.

The position of Merton and the other empirical functionalists does not advance the notion that the performance of certain specific functions is essential for the continued existence of a social structure. Merton simply looks at specific problems and proposes that an analytic viewpoint emphasizing function provides a potentially productive perspective for the analysis of social phenomena.

The concept of function has also been used in conjunction with an elaborate and provocative conceptual framework analysis.[33] Indeed, the borrowing of structural–functional analysis from the disciplines of sociology and anthropology has created most of the controversy concerning the use of function in political science during the past decade.

Structural–functional analysis is a widely discussed, if controversial, framework within the discipline of political science; however, the controversy is much less intense than in the 1960s, when some political scientists suggested that this model could provide the basis for an all-encompassing theory of politics.[34] It continues to be a central focus of sociological theory.

Structural functionalists believe that it is possible to identify certain basic functions which are requisite or essential for the survival of any social system. That is, a society that did not perform these basic essential functions would cease to survive as a society.

The precise number of requisite functions varies with the theorist consulted. Marion J. Levy, Jr., has suggested nine functional requisites.[35] Talcott Parsons, the guiding light of most political science functionalists, lists four functional requisites: pattern maintenance, goal attainment, adaption to the environment, and integration.[36]

Pattern Maintenance In Parsons's view, a society is a network of self-sufficient, interrelated roles that persist over time. It is a division of labor in which each role contributes to the persistence and self-sufficiency of the whole. Societies, however, are inherently unequal. Whether "value" is measured in terms of wealth, status, honor, or power, some individuals and groups invariably claim a larger share of socially desired values than others. To avoid having the established distribution of role and rewards shattered by competition over the unequal distribution of values, and to assure that the established social patterns will persist beyond the lifetime of a single generation, every society must make certain that its members accept and conform to the established rules of society. This process, referred to as pattern maintenance, involves at least three subprocesses: (1) socializing new members of society to believe in and to accept the established distribution of roles and rewards as just, (2) providing for the punishment of individuals who violate established norms, and (3) providing accepted mechanisms for the resolution of disputes and the displacement of tension.[37]

Pattern maintenance depends largely on establishing and maintaining a set of beliefs or a myth that justifies the existing structure of society and prescribes the way members of that society should behave if they are to be accepted as valued members. Such a set of beliefs is generally referred to as *culture.* (The concepts of culture and political culture are treated extensively in Chapter 4.)

Goal attainment   At least theoretically, individuals form societies to achieve certain goals. Without the attainment of the minimal goals of defense, sustenance, and a suitable environment for procreation, a society could neither be maintained nor persist. Whether societies possess goals beyond defense, sustenance, and procreation is an open question.

Adaption   If a society must meet certain goals to survive, it follows that it must continue to meet those goals even in the face of changing environmental circumstances. Societies that cannot adapt, cannot survive.

Integration   A society has been defined as a division of labor in which each role or group of roles, such as families or other structures, contributes to the persistence and self-sufficiency of the whole. Integration refers to the overall "fit" or congruence of the structures and culture of a society. A society in which the different roles are poorly coordinated, for example, would experience more difficulty in performing the pattern maintenance, goal attainment, and adaptation function than a society in which all the roles meshed into a highly synchronized whole. Without a minimal level of structural integration, the other functions could not be performed at all. In a similar manner, the more individuals have been socialized to believe in the utility and legitimacy of existing roles and structures, the more likely they are to play their roles in a manner conducive to the maintenance of existing social patterns. The complex structural arrangements such as the Indian Caste System, for example, could work efficiently only as long as individuals in all castes believed that the existing distribution of roles and rewards was divinely inspired. Once members of the lower castes began to make excessive demands for a redistribution of wealth and other valuables, their role performance changed, and the integration of the structural integration of Hindu society declined.[38] Thus for a society to be integrated, congruence must exist between structure and behavior. Rules are meaningless unless people abide by them.

The problems of integration, it should be noted, have been a persistent concern of political and social scientists, independent of the listing of integration as a functional requisite in structural-functional analysis.[39]

In addition to four main functions, Parsons also suggested that all societies share certain characteristics, the two most important being interdependence and equilibrium.[40] *Interdependence* refers to the assumption that all components in society are in some way connected, and when one component changes, all others will also change. Thus from the perspective of the political scientists, the introduction of economic and technological changes in the developing areas must inevitably produce changes in the political system. The challenge is to discover how!

The concept of *equilibrium*, as used in structural–functional analysis, indicates that all societies and components of societies are designed to maintain their existing form and to resist change. Once a society has achieved a sufficient degree of integration and has attained its goals to the satisfaction of its members, change poses a threat to all individuals in society and will be resisted. Perhaps more salient is the tendency of individuals in society occupying favored or elite positions to perceive change as a threat to their position and to actively seek to build stability or equilibrium into the cultural framework. Structures and behavior that maintain the equilibrium of a society are said to be functional or eufunctional. Those that impair the equilibrium of a society are dysfunctional. Equilibrium is used by other social scientists to mean that a society will always tend toward integration or at least harmony among its component parts. The central element in both definitions is the notion that societies will maximize stability.

Both equilibrium and interdependence, it must be stressed, are assumptions. Structural functionalists do not attempt to demonstrate empirically that all societies are characterized by interdependence, and tendencies toward equilibrium they accept as given.

The case for the utility of structural–functional analysis as a tool for political analysis has been clearly summarized by Gabriel A. Almond, one of its chief practitioners:

Even in this starkly simple form, the generic system model has value for the study of politics. The concept of function pushes us into realism and away from normative or ideological definitions. To answer functional questions we have to observe what a particular social system actually is and does. The concepts of functionality and dysfunctionality sensitize us to the factors making for social stability and social change, and enable us to perceive them in an orderly and thorough way. The concept of interdependence forces us to examine the performance of any structure or institution systematically; i.e., in all of its ramifications and interdependencies. We can no longer be contented with describing a single institution or looking at bilateral interactions. Our research must assume interdependence and interaction among all components.[41]

THE STRUCTURAL–FUNCTIONAL ANALYSIS OF POLITICAL SYSTEMS

Finding structural–functional analysis a useful framework for comparing societies, Almond and other political scientists have attempted to adapt structural–functional analysis to the specific requirements of comparative political analysis.

In this regard, Almond suggested that every political system must perform at least seven functions if it is to survive.[42] He lists these as:

INPUT FUNCTIONS
1. Political socialization and recruitment
2. Interest articulation
3. Interest aggregation
4. Political communication

OUTPUT FUNCTIONS
5. Rule making
6. Rule application
7. Rule adjudication

Political Socialization and Recruitment   For a political system to be effective in governing a society, it must inculcate members of the society with attitudes and values supportive of the system. (Socialization and the related concept of political culture are major areas of political research independent of their use in the structural–functional framework.) Recruitment refers to the need to induce new members to assume established political roles. Recruitment would appear to be a separate function, but Almond suggests that it is an extension of socialization:

The political recruitment function takes up where the general political socialization function leaves off. It recruits members of the society out of particular subcultures—religious communities, status classes, ethnic communities, and the like—and inducts them into the specialized roles of the political system, trains them in the appropriate skills, provides them with political cognitive maps, values, expectations, and affects.[43]

Interest Articulation   Political systems, as the earlier discussion of systems analysis suggested, are arrangements for converting demands into policy. For a political system to operate, therefore, it must provide means for the members of the society to make known their demands or "interests." This process is the interest articulation function.

Interest Aggregation   It is not sufficient for members of a society merely to be provided with the means to place "input" or demands into the political system. Individual and group demands tend to be narrow, sporadic, uncoordinated, and extremely difficult for the political system to come to grips with. For the political system to function effectively, the random and narrow demands of the polity must be collected, coordinated, and presented to the political system in a manageable package. This process is referred to as the interest aggregation function. The several thousand pressure groups in the United States, for example, articulate specific interests. The Democratic and Republican parties aggregate interests.

Communication   The communication function refers to the necessity of the political system to provide information to the polity concerning the "rules of the game"—how they should behave, and why they should value and continue to support the system. Communication also involves receiving information or feedback from the polity relating to demands and supports. All facets of political activity would cease without communication.

Rule Making, Rule Application, and Rule Adjudication   The output functions of rule making, application, and adjudication are named because to maintain itself, every society must make and apply decisions and provide means for settling disputes among its members. The making and administering of decisions and the judging of disputes, long the central focus of political science, require little elaboration.

The structural–functional analysis of political systems offers the comparative political scientist several advantages. First, it shifts the emphasis of analysis away from the largely sterile effort of comparing the political structures of different societies and toward the more important question of asking how different institutional arrangements handle certain problems (functions). For example, in attempting to compare the political institutions of the United States with those of the Soviet Union or Uganda in purely structural terms, we could do little but note that their political structures are more or less complex (differentiated). By focusing on functions rather than structures, however, one can also examine how different structural arrangements perform the same essential functions. This, in turn, allows the political scientist to compare the efficiency of different political systems in performing similar functions. It might be found, for example, that the Soviet Union is more efficient than the United States in socializing its citizens and that, accordingly, the Soviet Union will experience less internal stress in the years to come. Or, it might be found that the socialization, interest articulation, and interest aggregation mechanisms in Ethiopia cannot cope with the dislocations of economic change, such that the country's political system will not be able to effectively manage the larger social functional requisites of pattern maintenance and adaptation. On this basis, one might be able to predict that the established pattern of social equilibrium of Ethiopia will be shattered and that Ethiopia will undergo severe political and social stress until a new basis for social equilibrium can be established.

A second and related advantage is that structural–functional analysis focuses on the interaction and reciprocity between structures and functions. All political systems, by definition, perform all the requisite functions. A direct correlation exists, however, between the complexity of the function performed and the complexity of the structure required. In a remote African tribe, for example, the rule-making, rule-application, and rule-adjudication functions may be performed by the tribal chief. Quite clearly, a very simple structure is capable of performing the three output functions at only the most rudimentary level. If the size of the tribe were suddenly expanded, or if the members of the tribe were to suddenly demand more services, the existing structural arrangements would have to increase in complexity or the integration of the tribe would be jeopardized by the tribe's structural inability to see to the performance of the requisite functions. In the same manner, the ability of many developing areas to achieve the modernization goals desired by their leaders is severely impaired by the absence of adequate structures to perform the desired functions. A congruence, then, must exist between the type and levels of functions performed and the structural capability to perform those functions. Where such congruence does not exist, one can predict that the functions will be imperfectly performed.

A third advantage of structural–functional analysis is that it provides a means of visualizing the political process, as a whole as well as the relation of the component parts to the whole. In attempting to compare French and American political parties, for example, a structural functionalist would suggest that the investigator establish how the French and American political systems perform their requisite functions and then ascertain the role of political parties within the overall system. Following this procedure, it would be possible to compare not only differences in party structure but also differences in the functions performed by political parties in the two countries. It might even be concluded that expectations that the party systems were to perform different functions resulted in their having radically different structures.

For all its advantages, structural–functional analysis is primarily a *heuristic* rather than an empirical conceptual framework.[44] Just as the physicist finds the concept of "perfect vacuum" useful in conceptualizing problems dealing with vacuums, political scientists and sociologists have found it useful to *assume* that *all* societies perform certain functions and that *all* societies tend toward equilibrium. Most political scientists using structural–functional analysis ask such analytical questions as, How does the society I am analyzing perform its requisite functions? or, How does the political system I am analyzing perform its requisite functions? They then proceed to describe how the functions are performed, assuming that the society or the political systems is actually performing those functions, no more and no less. The assumption is not subjected to empirical research.

A related problem is the assumed interdependence of the components of social and political systems. Existing frameworks do not indicate how, in which direction, or under what circumstances changes in one part of the system will produce changes in other parts of the system or in the performance of the system as a whole. All that is said is that change produces change. No less disturbing is the implied equality between components of the system. Let us return the biologic analogy from which the concept of functional interdependence was originally derived. We know that the body can readily function without a finger, but not without a heart. Can we speak in the same way of the components of a social or a political sytem?

Structural–functional analysis can also be criticized on the grounds that its assumption of equilibrium predisposes researchers to look for equilibrium rather than change. If something is assumed to move toward equilibrium, the argument runs, most researchers will actively search for equilibrium and stability and will interpret their data, much of which may be ambiguous, to sustain the assumption that the drive toward equilibrium does indeed exist. Thus societies may be seen as possessing a far stronger drive toward equilibrium than empirically exists, and equally persistent tendencies toward change may be discounted or overlooked.

The foregoing criticisms notwithstanding, structural–functional analysis must be accorded considerable utility as a heuristic device to assist individual researchers to conceptualize social and political problems. It provides a loose framework for seeing how things fit together. It has also made the discipline as a whole more conscious of the interdependence of political phenomena and the interrelationship between political, social, and economic phenomena.

To go beyond its status as an heuristic framework, structural–functional analysis must be shifted from an a priori foundation to an empirical foundation. Requisite functions and assumptions of equilibrium and interdependence need to be empirically validated. Before this task can be seriously approached, advocates of structural–functional analysis must cope with the basic problems of definitional clarity and precision that beset virtually all general sociological concepts. It is to a general critique of these problems that we turn next.

CRITIQUE

Sociological concepts such as role, group, class, elite, structure, equilibrium, and function have profound explanatory value for political scientists. Indeed, they have become an integral part of political analysis. Therefore, it is particularly important for the political researcher to be aware of their weaknesses as well as their strengths.

Especially problematic is the multiplicity of meanings conveyed by each concept. The simple term "role," for example, is often used without qualifiers to express no less than 11 specialized meanings: individual role, aggregate role, behavior role, target role, overt role, covert role, prescriptive role, descriptive role, evaluating role, active role, and sanctioning role. Elaboration of these terms exceeds the scope of the present discussion, but we note that serious application of role analysis to political phenomena must come to grips with the concept's complexities and ambiguities. Similar examples could be provided for each of the major concepts discussed in this chapter. Function, for instance, is used by social scientists to specify: (1) acts or actions a structure is designed to perform; (2) any service performed by a social structure, intended (manifest) or accidental (latent); (3) all activities of a social structure, whether they strengthen society (are eufunctional or functional) or weaken it (are dysfunctional); (4) any process that a society must perform successfully if it is to survive (requisite functions).

All the concepts discussed in this chapter are hard to define with precision. A social structure, for example, was said to be an established pattern of human interaction that persists over time. At precisely what point do human interactions become structured? How long and under what circumstances must they persist? At what point can they be recognized? Such problems are particularly evident in attempts to define the boundaries of groups. How do we decide who belongs to the Republican or Democratic party? Only card-carrying members? Anyone who claims to be a party member? Anyone who voted for party members over a span of more than three elections? Anyone who usually votes for the party? Again, problems of boundary ambiguity beset virtually every sociological concept, those relating to function as well as those connected with structure. The terms eufunctional and dysfunctional refer to system-supportive and system-destructive functions, respectively. But how does one know whether certain functions are eufunctional or dysfunctional? Is conflict dysfunctional? If so, what kinds and how much? Also, if some forms and levels of conflict are eufunctional, is it to be assumed that the same types and levels of conflict are functional for all societies at all times? Or, does the functionality of conflict vary from society to society and within the same society over time?

The presence of diffuse and imprecise boundaries has also led to severe problems in the operationalization of structural concepts. Function-related concepts are also difficult to empirically operationalize. Short of an all-out collapse, how can we tell until long after the fact, if at all, whether a society is moving away from an established position of equilibrium, or has passed a threshold and is moving toward a new equilibrium? What indicators would be used? Indeed, can it be empirically demonstrated that societies move toward a state of equilibrium? Perhaps societies are constantly in a state of flux, and periods of low activity are misinterpreted as equilibrium.

In addition to problems of definitional clarity and operationalization, the political scientist should bear in mind that the boundaries of social structures and functions often vary markedly from society to society.[45] For example, the boundaries of the middle class(es) in Latin American countries are not the same as the boundaries of middle class(es) in the United States, nor are their attributes and political values necessarily the same. Similarly, the composition of elites varies not only from country to country, but even among regions within the same country. Concepts such as role or class may be assumed to be universal in their application, but the definition of their boundaries is a separate empirical question for each specific region.

The existence of social structures does not confer on them political relevance. Because pressure groups have access to governmental agencies, they do not necessarily have influence with those agencies. Because social class correlates with high levels of political involvement, it cannot be assumed that class structure is the cause of high involvement. High levels of education and high incomes, also associated with high levels of political involvement, may be the primary causal factors. Thus the correlation between class and participation could be incidental.

Finally, the problem of levels of generality must be kept in mind. Characteristics of groups cannot be directly imputed to group members. Because working-class status correlates highly with low education, it cannot be assumed that each member of the working class is poorly educated. The behavior and attributes of individuals as individuals is not identical with the behavior and attributes of individuals as collectives.

SUMMARY

The concepts of sociology have been particularly useful in enabling the political scientist to analyze political processes and institutions as social entities rather than legal artifacts. Indeed, the boundaries separating the two disciplines have become increasingly blurred. However, as concepts adapted from sociology have provided political scientists with powerful tools for analyzing and conceptualizing the political process, they have also confronted them with the problems of clarity, precision, operationalization, and measurement inherent in most social theory.

NOTES

[1] Seymour Martin Lipset, *Political Man* (Garden City, N.Y.: Doubleday, 1960), p. 23.

[2] For an extended discussion of social structure see: Marion J. Levy, Jr., *The Structure of Society* (Princeton, N.J.: Princeton University Press, 1952); also see Robert K. Merton, *Social Theory and Social Structure* New York: Free Press, 1957).

[3] William Shakespeare, *As You Like It*, act II, scene 7.

[4] J. Milton Yinger, *Toward a Field Theory of Behavior* (New York: McGraw-Hill, 1965) chap. 6; also see Bruce J. Biddle and Edwin J. Thomas, eds., *Role Theory: Concepts and Research* (New York: Wiley, 1966).

[5] Biddle and Thomas, Role Theory, chapter II, pp. 23–45.

[6] Ralph K. Huitt, "Democratic Party Leadership in the Senate," *American Political Science Review* (1961, pp. 333–344; Huitt, "The Morse Committee Assignment Controversy: A Study in Senate Norms," *American Political Science Review* (1957), pp. 313–329; Donald R. Matthews, "The Folkways of the United States Senate: Conformity to Group Norms and Legislative Effectiveness," *American Political Science Review*, (1959), pp. 1064–1089.

[7] John C. Wahlke, Heinz Eulau, William Buchanan, and Leroy C. Ferguson, *The Legislative System* (New York: Wiley, 1962).

[8] Arthur F. Bentley, *The Process of Government* (Chicago: University of Chicago Press, 1908).

[9] David B. Truman, *The Governmental Process* (New York: Knopf, 1951) pp. 32–34. For a survey of sociological research on groups see Dorwin Cartwright and Alvin Zander, eds., *Group Dynamics*, 3rd ed. (New York: Harper & Row, 1968).

[10] Truman, *The Governmental Process*, p. 264.

[11] Lewis A. Froman, Jr., "Some Effects of Interest Group Strength in State Politics," *American Political Science Review*, vol. 60, no. 4 (December 1966), p. 961.

[12] Robert L. Ross, "Relations Among National Interest Groups," *Journal of Politics*, vol. 32, no. 1 (February, 1970), pp. 96–114.

[13] Robert J. Lieber, "Interest Groups and Political Integration: British Entry into Europe," *American Political Science Review*, vol. 66, no. 1, (March 1972), pp. 53–67.

[14] Joseph LaPalombara, "The Utility and Limitations of Interest Group Theory in Non-American Field Situations," *Journal of Politics*, vol. 22 (1960), pp. 29–49.

[15] Robert F. Bales, *Interaction Process Analysis* (Cambridge, Mass.: Harvard University Press, 1950), p. 3.

[16] Cartwright and Zander, eds., *Group Dynamics.*

[17] Ronald Lippitt and Ralph K. White "An Experimental Study of Leadership and Group Life," *Readings in Social Psychology*, Guy Swanson, Theodore Newcomb, and Eugene Hartley, eds. (New York: Holt, 1952).

[18] For example, see: Thomas J. Cook, James W. Dyson; and L. Douglas Dobson, "Learning as a Component of Political Socialization," *Experimental Study of Politics*, forthcoming.

[19] Sidney Verba, *Small Groups and Political Behavior: A Study of Leadership* (Princeton, N.J.; Princeton University Press, 1961).

[20] For general discussions of social stratification, see: Tomotsu Shibutani and Kian M. Kwan, *Ethnic Stratification* (New York: Macmillan, 1965); George E. Simpson and J. Milton Yinger, *Racial and Cultural Minorities* (New York: Harper & Row, 1965). Cynthia H. Enloe, *Ethnic Conflict and Political Development* (Boston: Little, Brown, 1973). Robert A. Levine, and Donald T. Campbell, *Ethnocentrism: Theories of Conflict, Ethnic Attitudes, and Group Behavior* (New York: Wiley, 1972).

[21] Alex Inkeles, "Social Stratification and Mobility in the Soviet Union: 1940–1950," *American Sociological Review*, vol. 15, no. 4, (August 1950), pp. 465–479.

[22] Lipset, *Political Man*, pp. 223–224.

[23] Thomas R. Dye and L. Harmon Zeigler, *The Few and the Many* (Belmont, Calif.; Duxbury, 1972).

[24] Truman, *The Governmental Process*; Robert A. Dahl, *Who Governs?* (New Haven: Conn.; Yale University Press, 1961).

[25] Charles Beard, *An Economic Interpretation of the Constitution* (New York: MacMillan, 1913); William Domhoff, *Who Rules America?* (Englewood Cliffs, N.J.; Prentice-Hall, 1967); Floyd Hunter, *Community Power Structure* (Chapel Hill: University of North Carolina Press, 1953); C. Wright Mills, *The Power Elite* (New York: Oxford University Press, 1956).

[26] Joseph LaPalombara "Political Science and the Engineering of National Development," in Monte Palmer and Larry Stern, *Political Development and Changing Societies* (Lexington, Mass.: Heath, 1971), pp. 27–66.

[27] For example, see: Bruce Russet, *International Regions and the International System* (Skokie, Ill.: Rand McNally, 1967); Amitai Etzioni, *Political Unification* (New York: Holt, Rinehart & Winston, 1965); J. S. Nye, *Peace in Parts* (Boston: Little, Brown, 1971); Karl W. Deutsch et al., *Political Community and the North Atlantic Area* (Princeton, N.J.: Princeton University Press, 1957).

[28] William Flanagan and Edwin Fogelman, "Functionalism in Political Science," in Don Martindale, ed., *Functionalism in the Social Sciences* (Philadelphia: The American Academy of Political and Social Science, 1965) pp. 111, 126.

[29] Ibid.

[30] Ibid., p. 113.

[31] Merton, *Social Theory and Social Structure*, chap. 1.

[32] Ibid.

[33] In anthropology, Bronislaw Malinowski and A. R. Radcliffe-Brown were extremely influential. Among sociologists, Talcott Parsons and Marion J. Levy, Jr., have had great influence. The work of these four is most

sophisticated and most often cited by political scientists. The claims and aims advanced in the early enthusiasm associated with this concept have not all come to fruition, and controversies have developed.

[34] For examples of applications of this type of analysis, see William C. Mitchell, *The American Polity* (New York: Free Press, 1967); and Robert T. Holt and John E. Turner, *The Political Basis of Economic Development* (New York: Van Nostrand Reinhold, 1966). Gabriel A. Almond and James S. Coleman, eds., *The Politics of Developing Areas* (Princeton, N.J.: Princeton University Press, 1960). See introduction.

[35] Marion J. Levy, Jr., *The Structure of Society* (Princeton, N.J.: Princeton University Press, 1952), pp. 149 ff.

[36] Talcott Parsons, *Economy and Society* (New York: Free Press, 1956) pp. 16 ff.

[37] Robert T. Holt, "A Proposed Structural-Functional Framework for Political Science," in Martindale, *Functionalism in Political Science*, pp. 84–110.

[38] Harold R. Isaacs, *India's Ex-Untouchables* (New York: John Day, 1965).

[39] Philip E. Jacob and James V. Toscano, *The Integration of Political Communities* (Philadelphia: Lippincott, 1964); Claude Ake, *A Theory of Political Integration* (Homewood, Ill.: Dorsey, 1967).

[40] Levy, *The Structure of Society*; Parsons, *Economy and Society.*

[41] Gabriel A. Almond, "A Developmental Approach to Political Systems," *World Politics*, (January 1965) p. 186. Copyright © 1965 by Princeton University Press; reprinted by permission.

[42] Almond and Coleman, eds., *Politics of Developing Areas, Introductory Essay.*

[43] Ibid.

[44] Martin Landau, *Political Theory and Political Science* (New York: Macmillan, 1972); see especially, "On the Use of Functional Analysis in American Political Science."

[45] Stanislaw Ossowski, *Different Conceptions of Social Class* (London: Routledge & Kegan Paul, 1963) pp. 121–144.

4

Anthropology and Politics

For most of their respective histories, political science and anthropology have occupied opposite ends of the social science spectrum. Political scientists studied the formal political institutions of economically developed states in the Western hemisphere; anthropologists were primarily interested in the social and cultural patterns of the world's preliterate societies, especially those of Africa and the Americas. For the most part, the two disciplines were mutually irrelevant.

Since World War II, however, changes within both anthropology and political science have opened several areas of mutual interest. Anthropologists turned their attention to the analysis of peasant societies as well as more rudimentary forms of primitive life. They also produced excellent studies exploring the susceptibilty and resistance of diverse forms of traditional society to the onslaught of modern technology. Finally, anthropologists actively sought closer ties with the social science disciplines, including political science, in an effort to enhance their analyses of traditional societies.[1]

From the political science perspective, the end of World War II brought an immediate and profound interest in what were termed "non-Western" or developing areas. This interest intensified as former colonies sought their independence, and particularly as the "Third World" became the arena of cold war conflict. In seeking information relating to the structure of traditional societies, the mechanics of their political relationships, and their resistance to acculturation of Western political forms and ideologies, political scientists were forced to "discover" the world of anthropology.

Moreover, if political scientists are to develop models of political behavior that are universally applicable, they will eventually be obliged to extend their models to cover primitive as well as modern political relationships. Again, political scientists will logically rely on the information and techniques of the anthropologist in this effort.

Along the same line, it could be argued that observations of primitive political behavior and relationships would be the logical starting point for building more complex models of political behavior. At least intuitively, it would seem to be easier to observe political relationships in the simple and highly visible environment of the primitive society than in the tangled morass of modern industrial societies.

Relating the concepts of anthropology to political research brings up two problems. First, in spite of the increasing areas of shared interest between the two disciplines, few political scientists have drawn heavily on anthropological resources. Thus it is easier to discuss the relevance of anthropological concepts than to illustrate their application by political scientists.

The second problem involves the affinity of the disciplines of anthropology and sociology. Their basic concepts, particularly those of greatest relevance to political analysis, are either similar or identical. For example, the origins and development of structural–functional requisite analysis lie as much in the works of anthropologists such as Bronislaw Malinowski as in the theories of Talcott Parsons.

To avoid needless duplication of the concepts covered in Chapter 3 and to focus on the areas of anthropological research of greatest relevance to political science, this discussion is limited to the concepts "primitive" and "culture" and their derivatives. "Primitive" and "culture," it should be noted, are the two central or organizing concepts of anthropological research.

PRIMITIVE SOCIETIES

As used by anthropologists, the term "primitive" is both complex and imprecise. As Melville J. Herskowits suggests, it is probably incapable of operationalization. As presented in its classical form, the primitive society is preliterate (i.e., it has no written language).[2] Its social structures are based solely on kinship and are seldom more sophisticated than the tribe. Its economic activities require minimal specialization and are generally limited to hunting, herding, and rudimentary forms of agriculture. In political terms, authority may be exercised by a chief and elders, or, as in the case of the Logoli, the Tallensi, and the Nuer, the society may be without recognizable forms of authority.[3] On the religious dimension, primitives are highly superstitious, and all facets of life are related or attributable to supernatural forces. In behavioral terms, they are variously described as noninnovative, fatalistic, and prescientific in their thought. They are also present oriented—that is, concerned only with immediate events and gratifications.[4] The expression "shame culture" has also been applied, inasmuch as the primary means of social control is fear of exposure by neighbors rather than internalized feelings of guilt. Primitive loyalty patterns are centered on the extended family and seldom exceed the tribe. Some feeling for the primitve's social world can be gleaned from the diagram of Nuer loyalty patterns presented in Figure 4.1.

Finally, two of the most obvious distinguishing characteristics of primitive societies are their isolation and their apparent changlessness. In these remote and self-sustaining areas, established forms of social interaction persist from generation to generation until changes in the environment cause the society to perish, either through natural disaster or because of the incursions of the more "civilized" world.

The unwillingness of anthropologists to allow the term "primitive" to convey the impression of condescension or disdain has been expressed by Manning Nash:

A word of apology is needed for the use of "primitive" and "peasant" as labels for either societies or economies. I do not mean by "primitive" either archaic, or less than fully human, nor even doomed to destruction. "Primitive" is a catchword and refers to a host of small, nonmonetized, non-Western societies and economies. This label has become familiar through usage, and it does summon up images of what kinds of things I hoped to describe and analyze in this study. "Primitive" is not a scientifically meaningful word when applied to societies and cultures, and I do not use it for theoretical or analytical ends, but merely as a banner, a device to call up associations.[5]

Peasants   In recent years the interest of many anthroppologists has shifted from the study of primitive societies to the study of peasant societies. In so doing they have moved

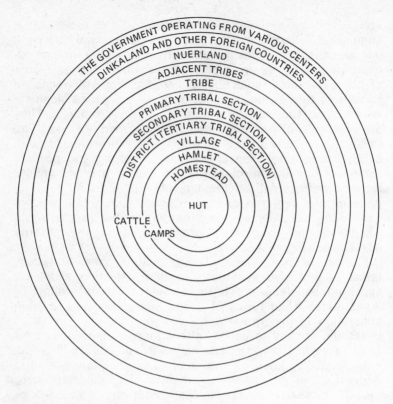

Figure 4.1   Nuer loyalty patterns.
(Sudan Notes and Records, 1933–1938 in M. Fortes and
E. E. Evans-Pritchard, eds., *African Political Systems*,
published for The International African Institute by
Oxford University Press. Copyright 1940.)

from an investigation of remote groups that form but a small
fraction of humanity to a consideration of what is perhaps
the predominant form of social organization in the world
today. Clearly a majority of the populations of Asia, Africa,
and Latin America appear to fall in or close to the peasant
category.

   The difference between primitive and peasant societies
seems to have originated in the pattern of economic distribution. As discussed by Eric R. Wolf:

Thus, in primitive societies producers control the means of production, including their own labor, and exchange their own labor and its products for the culturally defined equivalent goods and services of others. In the course of cultural evolution, however, such simple systems have been superseded by others in which control of the means of production, including the disposition of human labor, passes from the hands of the primary producers, into the hands of groups that do not carry on the productive process themselves, but assume instead special executive and administrative functions, backed by the use of force. The constitution of society in such a case is no longer based on equivalent and direct exchanges of goods and services between one group and another; rather, goods and services are first furnished to a center and only later redirected. In primitive society, surpluses are exchanged directly among groups or members of groups; peasants, however, are rural cultivators whose surpluses are transferred to a dominant group of rulers that uses the surpluses both to underwrite its own standards of living and to distribute the remainder to groups in society that do not farm but must be fed for their specific goods and services in return.[6]

The peasant, then, is forced to provide for society as well as for the needs of his own family. He must pay rent in the form of surpluses on the land he farms. Yet in spite of his added burden, the levels of technology and the forms of social organization he achieves differ little from those of the primitive. The plot of land that he share-crops is run as a kinship household rather than as a business.[7] All members of the kin group work in the field at essentially the same task performed by other families in the village. Division of labor either within or among families is minimal. In their all-consuming effort to pay the rent and yet eke out a subsistence for their familes—approximately 2000 calories per person per day—the peasant is literally ground into the earth. In many of the predominantly peasant areas of the world, for example, the current daily caloric intake is well below the 2000-calorie level.[8]

Moreover, the cards seem to be perpetually stacked against the peasant. If he prospers, his less fortunate kin immediately make demands on his surplus; and because the kinship unit is his primary source of security and social interaction, he finds it difficult to refuse. In addition, the exigencies of peasant life make children, particularly males, a necessity. They help in the fields, enhance the family's power vis à vis its neighbors, provide security in old age, and stand as visible testimony to the father's virility. They also represent additional mouths to feed, rendering the prospects of a surplus even more remote. If surpluses nevertheless occur, virtually all peasant cultures provide for what economic anthropologists refer to as *leveling devices.* To impress one's neighbors—a pervasive concern in peasant cultures—births, circumcisions, weddings, holy days, and deaths must be celebrated with grand display, even at the price of placing a marginally prosperous family forever in debt to the landlord and perpetuating its serfdom. A short but cogent discussion of these and simlar relationships can be found in Manning Nash's *Primitive and Peasant Economic Systems.*[9]

Just as the peasant is indebted to the landlord or overlord for his plot of land, he must rely on the overlord for intercession with the outside world. If the peasant runs afoul of the law or requires government services, he turns first to the landlord. The landlord is his *patron.* In return for the patron's intercession, the peasant surrenders his political rights. If elections are held, he is expected to vote for the landlord. In local conflicts, he is the landlord's militia. As Gideon Sjøberg points out, peasant society is essentially a feudal society.[10]

This is not to suggest that the peasant is devoted to or particularly enamored of the patron. His dependency relationship leaves no choice. In the peasant's perception of the world, the patron is all-powerful while he, the peasant, is powerless. Acts of disloyalty are severely punished, even to the point of forcing the peasant off the land. To be forced off the land is to be exiled from the kinship groups on which the peasant is dependent for virtually everything he values, to be uprooted from ancestral ties, and to be without visible means of livelihood.

Aside from the economic distinction, and even though peasant societies are often clustered together rather than isolated from one another, peasant and primitive societies appear to have much in common. The extended family, including cousins several times removed, continues to be the primary form of social organization and is the center of the individual's universe. Among other things, the family is the primary unit of labor, the primary agent of socialization, the primary unit of security in conflict situations, the primary unit of succor in illness or old age, the primary source of friendship and recreational associations, and even the primary avenue of mate selection. Whether the mate is selected endogamously (within the extended family network) or exogenously (outside the kinship network), the mediating influence of the family is paramount. It is little wonder that the peasant's loyalties are centered at the family and kinship levels and seldom beyond. It should be noted that the larger structural units of peasant societies, such as the clan and the tribe, are essentially aggregates of extended families. In most tribes, at least mythically, all members are descendants of the same ancestor. Villages, too, tend to be composed of one or more related clans, with kinship ties being the predominant lines of cleavage in village politics and conflict.

Mention must also be made of the peasant's physical and demographic environment. Because he lives at subsistence level and can make little provison for future emergencies, the peasant is vulnerable to all natural disasters. Flood, drought, or pestilence can destroy his marginal existence. Furthermore, since peasants are largely illiterate, save for religious teachings, they are poorly equipped to cope with their misery in ways other than those dictated by tradition and local superstition. Landlords, for their part, generally equate education with unrest and resist efforts to abolish peasant illiteracy. Finally, most peasant populations are stricken with one, two, or even more debilitating diseases, ranging from tuberculosis to bilharzia. To borrow the words of Thomas Hobbes, peasant life, tends to be "nasty, dull, brutish, and short."

The peasant's social, cultural, and physical milieus have produced behavioral correlates that are common to most peasant areas if not universal in their applicability. Preeminently, the peasant is fatalistic. Everything that happens is the work of God, fate, or the spirits. His faith in human volition is negligible. Similarly, he has been socialized to disdain innovation. As David Riesman wrote, the peasant is socialized "to succeed his father rather than to succeed."[11] Peasants are also intensely suspicious, distrustful, and insecure in relation to their neighbors. Life, according to some anthropologists, is a struggle simultaneously to keep the neighbors in their place while dodging their scorn. Some feeling for this situation is provided by the following description of peasant animosities in southern Italy.

The peasants of Stefanaconi are given to suspicion, quarrels, vituperation, abuse, violence, and conflicts of all sorts. But what is more important . . . is that they are cognizant of the fact, and in moments of reflection they condemn themselves for it. They point out with horror that there is a "murder a year"; they inform with anger that theft, both in the village and in the country, is a disastrously common ocurrence; they point out with a mixture of shame and fear that it is virtually impossible to find an extended family without animosities which often last an adult lifetime. . . .

An artisan, a peasant man, and a peasant woman were interviewed about . . . the rumors concerning morals in Stefanaconi. Between the three of them they accused nearly a hundred women of adultery or fornication, a number which this writer considers extravagant. Interestingly enough, the two male informants counted themselves among the male partners to the alleged illicit sexual behavior, although the principal partners were reputed to be several leisurely signori and a number of distant relatives of the accused women themselves. . . .[12]

Peasants have also been found to be exceedingly conservative in outlook, manifesting deep reverence for the ways of tradition and equal suspicion of innovation and change. Governments are understandably viewed with doubt and misgiving, and kinship orientation does not permit feelings of nationalism: A peasant is a member of a clan, tribe, or village, not of a nation.

Peasant societies are also characterized by a sense of changelessness. New technology may enter the peasant's world through the agency of the landlord or the government, but his intense ties to the kinship group, his deep-rooted socialization into conforming and noninnovative behavior, his attitudes of doubt, suspicion, and insecurity, and his precarious existence all combine to produce a social and psychological edifice that is profoundly resistant to change.

Traditional Societies

Peasant and primitive societies, as well as societies in various stages of transition from primitive to peasant status, are collectively referred to as traditional societies, since both primitive and peasant societies are organized primarily along kinship lines, are largely without intense loyalty to non-kinship structures such as the state, and look to past traditions for the solutions to their problems rather than depending on innovation and readily accepting modern techniques. Most aspects of the models of primitive and peasant societies presented above are applicable to most primitive and peasant societies in the world. More extensive attempts to build a general model of traditional societies can be found in Everett E. Hagen's *Toward a Theory of Social Change* and Talcott Parsons's *Societies*.[13]

Political Anthropology and the Politics of Traditional Societies

The anthropologist's delineation of traditional societies has come to form the backbone of almost all political and social analyses of the developing areas. Four areas of political applicability, however, are particularly noteworthy. First, in understanding the politics of the world's least economically developed states, the only data available are, in most cases, anthropological data. With rare exceptions, political scientists have shown little interest in the world's least developed areas. Fortunately, this situation is now being remedied by the emergence of political anthropology as an established subfield of social anthropology. Political anthropological studies have not only delineated various forms of authority patterns found in traditional societies, they have equally stressed the roles of such cultural variables as religion, superstition, magic, rituals, and ancestral ties in providing a legitimate base for traditional political systems. Such political systems are said to be based largely on ascription (i.e., positions are obtained because of lineage and social status rather than achievement). Moreover, although traditional economic systems may be dysfunctional in terms of producing large economic surpluses, they are very functional in maintaining the stability of traditional power relationships. Highly productive economic systems, for instance, generally require norms that stress innovation, equality, and advancement based on achievement rather than ascription. They also require specialized divisions of labor utilizing the rational ordering of production roles rather than kinship units such as the extended family. It is questionable, indeed, whether political relationships based on ascription, inequality, and

kinship could long endure in the same society in which economic relationships were based on achievement, equality,
and the non-kin, rational ordering of kinship roles. Political
anthropologists, in short, have attempted to demonstrate
that the characteristic stability of traditional political orders
is based on the compatibilty or integration of all aspects of
society—social structure, culture, political system, economic
systems, and environment or ecosystem. One of the pioneer-
ing works in this area was Fortes and Evans-Pritchard's
African Political Systems, first published in 1940.[14]

The anthropological model of traditional societies is essential to understanding the behavior of the segments, even of
rapidly developing states, that continue to resist modernization. The populations of most developing areas fall roughly
into three groups: a modern-oriented, well-educated segment that lives largely in the urban areas and comprises
much of the middle and upper class; a large rural population
that consists of peasant cultivators organized along the
lines of the traditional model; and a transitional segment
comprised of individuals caught in the changeover between
the traditional and the modern forms of society. To analyze
the difficulties experienced by modernizing leaders attempting to integrate their traditional populations into a viable
nation clearly requires an appreciation of the roots of the
traditional individual's loyalty to and dependence on the kinship groups as well as his social and psychological milieus.

One of the earliest and best studies of the impact of
traditional populations on national integration or national
building was David E. Apter's *Gold Coast in Transition*, later
revised as *Ghana in Transition*.[15] In particular, Apter's work
illustrates how support for Nkrumah's Convention Peoples'
party (CPP), the party of the independence movement, came
largely from areas of the Gold Coast that had experienced
substantial social and technological change and that the
greatest opposition to the CPP came from the heavily traditional tribal areas, and particularly those of the Ashanti.
Moreover, Apter found that much of the support the CPP
did receive in the largely traditional hinterlands was based
on traditional tribal conflicts and opposition to the dominant
position of the Ashanti rather than on support for Nkrumah
and his party.

In a second work, *The Political Kingdom*, Apter draws heavily on anthropological models of primitive authority patterns to illustrate the hypothesis that the ability of a traditional society to absorb and successfully accommodate change without doing irreparable damage to existing political arrangements depends on the level of differentiation of the primitive political and social structures.[16] He discovered that highly differentiated primitive societies (i.e., societies possessing a relatively complex division of political, social, and economic roles) absorbed and accommodated the incursions of modernization far better than did primitive societies whose political systems were organized along rigid hierarchical lines. The latter, it developed, were inflexibly opposed to modernization, and they collapsed under its relentless pressure. The former, exemplified by the Buganda of Uganda, were better able to bend and cope with modernization; accordingly, they maintained much of their traditional political and social structure intact.

A related application of anthropological research to political analysis lies in understanding the persistence of traditional attitudes and behavior patterns among populations that have long ago given up the traditional model of social organization. Migrants to the urban areas cling to their traditions and generally continue, wherever possible, to live in kinship or ethnic enclaves. Voting patterns and the allocation of bureaucratic associations in virtually all developing areas are heavily influenced by kinship, ethnic, religious, and other particularistic considerations. One of the clearest examples of this situation is the allocation of virtually all political positions in the Lebanese government, appointive or elective, on the basis of sectarian affiliation, even though Lebanon is clearly one of the most prosperous, Westernized, urbanized, and educated states in the Third World. Table 4.1, adapted from Elie Salem, displays the sectarian allocation of the Lebanese cabinet on the basis of the relative size and political importance of each sect.

The persistence of traditional attitudes and behavior patterns in new structural environments was labeled *cultural lag* by sociologist William F. Ogburn.[17] To understand why traditional values continue to be revered in modern or nonprimitive settings, Ogburn pointed out, requires compre-

Table 4.1   Patterns of Lebanese Cabinet Structure 1943–1961
(Omitting Abortive, Emergency or Interim Cabinets)

Size of Cabinet	6	8	9	10	10	10	14	17
Sunni	1	2	2	2	2	3	3	4
Maronite	1	2	2	3	3	3	3	4
Druze	1	1	2	2	1	1	2	2
Greek Orthodox	1	1	1	1	1	1	2	2
Greek Catholic	1	1	1	1	1	1	1	1
Shi i	1	1	1	1	2	1	2	3
Armenian Catholic							1	
Armenian Orthodox								1

Source: Elie Salem, "Cabinet Politics in Lebanon," *The Middle East Journal*, vol. 21, no. 4 (Autumn 1967), p. 499.

hension of the traditional socialization processes through which they were acquired, their role in ordering the life of the individual, and the intensity with which they were held by the individual. Again, anthropological studies provide the political scientist with data relevant to these queries. Such data also give us some knowledge of how the traditional institutions fulfilled the traditional individuals' needs for security, belonging, and affection, and what modern institutions must do to meet these needs. The more trouble modern societies have in trying to supply the needs of transitional populations, the more they are forced to rely on or to simulate traditional forms of need gratification. For example, we can assume that family loyalties remain intense in most developing areas partly because of their continued functionality. Even in economically developing societies the family plays a crucial role in aiding the individual economically, politically, and psychologically. Until modernizing societies can provide functional equivalents, many traditional behavior patterns, such as intense parochial loyalties, will persist long after the structural environment of the individual has acquired the overt trappings of modernization. This process is well reflected in such anthropological studies as Leonard Plotnicov's *Strangers to the City*, a study of urban adaption in Jos, Nigeria, and Oscar Lewis's *Five Families* and related works dealing with adaptation to change in Mexico and Latin America.[18]

Traditional–Modern Typologies

Finally, the anthropological delineation of traditional societies has become central to the political and social analysis of developing areas because it serves as the base point of typologies of political, economic, and social development. In presenting his theory of social evolution, the German sociologist Tonnies suggested there were two polar forms of social organization: *gemeinschaft* and *gesellschaft*.[19] *Gemeinschaft* societies, which approximate the traditional model outlined above, are based on kinship ties—the individual is born into the social unit, and neither his fitness for membership nor his sense of belonging is ever questioned; interpersonal relationships are emotional or affective. *Gesellschaft* societies are typified by the modern bureaucratic or industrial organization. Membership is selective and one's place is never certain but dictated by the changing, rational needs of the institution. Ties of kinship are irrelevant, and interpersonal relations are characterized by their formality and affective neutrality. According to Tonnies, society is in the process of evolving from the gemeinschaft to the gessellschaft.

Similarly, Max Weber posited three forms of social organization and authority: traditional, charismatic, and rational–legal.[20] As in the case of Tonnies's gemeinschaft and gesellschaft, Weber's traditional society corresponded to the traditional model presented here. The rational–legal model was patterned on Weber's concept of an ideal bureaucracy in which all positions would be filled on the basis of merit and organizational need, rather than the ties of kinship. In the charismatic society, we find personalized loyalties to highly magnetic individuals, such as Castro and Mao Tse-tung, who through their appeal to the masses lead the social transformation from traditional to modern.

One of the most recent attempts to establish a typology of traditional and modern societies is Talcott Parsons's delineation of "pattern variables of action orientation."[21] In Parsons's view it is insufficient to establish two or three ideal types and assume that all societies will more or less fit those categories. Rather, Parsons suggests that the contrast between modern and traditional societies should be examined along a multidimensional continuum. Specifically, he proposes to compare and evaluate societies on the basis of

five "pattern variables": ascription–achievement, particular-
ism–universalism, affectivity–affective neutrality, self-orien-
tation–collective orientation, and diffuseness–specificity. A
complete understanding of the fullness of the pattern variables requires careful reading of Parsons and Shils's
Toward a General Theory of Action.[22]

Very simply, *affectivity* refers to the tendency of traditional
individuals to view other individuals in emotional terms
heavily colored by personal values. Things do not have neutral status; they are either good or bad, right or wrong, desirable or undesirable, depending on the values of the individual.
The possibilty of other individuals behaving in a neutral and
disinterested manner is not recognized. The affective individual assumes that other people are going to put themselves and their own groups first and that he must therefore do the same. Conversely, the affectively neutral person
is willing to perceive other individuals and institutions as
neutral, disinterested, fair-minded, unbiased, and amenable
to playing by the rules.

Collectively oriented individuals consistently tend to play
by the rules—even when no one is watching—and consistently sacrifice personal values for the sake of the social or
community good. Traditional individuals on the other hand,
are consistently *self-oriented.* Compliance with traditional
norms flows more from fear of being humiliated or otherwise punished than from conscience or guilt feelings; abstract concern for the common good tends to be minimal
unless directly tied to more immediate individual or family
values.

Universality, as the word implies, refers to the uniform
application of rules to all individuals in a particular situation.
"All people are equal in the eyes of the law," is a universalistic statement. Traditional societies, however, tend to be
particularistic. Members of one's family, clan, tribe, con-
fessional, ethnic group, or class are special and deserve
particular and favored treatment. Moreover, members of in-
groups expect preferential, particular treatment, and failure
to receive such treatment is grounds for conflict within
the group.

Achievement refers to the granting of status and authority
on the basis of demonstrated ability. Merit systems epitomize

selection by achievement. The tendency in traditional societies is to accord status, deference, and authority by *ascription*. Because of age, sex, birth lineage, or some supernatural connection, individuals are ascribed or credited with desirable virtues without being required to demonstrate their proficiency. The deference once accorded members of India's Brahman caste is probably the best-known illustration of ascription.

Specificity is exemplified by the precise (or specific) nature of modern legal and contractual systems. Specific obligations are codified and sharply defined. *Diffuse* rules, obligations, and ties are those of kinship and custom. In traditional societies, interaction between individuals is regulated by norms (accepted behavior standards) and not by explicitly defined codes.

Of the five variables, the self–collective orientation is the most ambiguous. Traditional societies are noted for their emphasis on the kin and primary group, yet individuals tend to act in very self-oriented ways. The following description of the Egyptian peasant illustrates this point.

Thus the village, united against the world, is divided against itself, and confidence and mistrust live side by side.

The passion of the fellahin for the soil unites them when it is threatened, and divides them as they own or covet it. The ideas of nation, patriotism, are foreign to the fellah, but the idea of cooperation, of public interest and of community life are no less so. The Egyptian village is not a community in the social sense, not an organism, but a mass.

Similarity in the mode of life, and propinquity, do not necessarily create deep human relations. A certain spiritual life is needed; or at least the influence of spiritual personalities, to make social relations possible. But the fellah does not develop as a spiritual personality. Absorbed in the soil and oppressed by those above him, he lives collectively but not socially. Although living in a herd, he remains at bottom isolated and solitary.

This absence of coordination between homogeneous elements has helped to maintain the Egyptian village and the peasant society in much the same state for fifty centuries. And for fifty centuries, governments have encouraged this formlessness, because it greatly strengthens their authority.[23]

Conversely, individuals in economically developed societies seem to be self-oriented in their pursuit of private gain, but they nevertheless show intense collective orientations in their loyalty to the state and in their manifestations of civic and social responsibilty. In many ways the self–collective dimension approximates the shame–guilt dimension mentioned earlier. Self-oriented individuals put the collective first only when the fear of being shamed is paramount. Collectively oriented indivduals, by contrast, are guilt ridden. They put the collective first because they have been taught to internalize the values of their society as their own. Because of the ambiguity associated with the self-collective dimension, however, it is often omitted from classifications of societies on the pattern variable framework.[24]

In summary, traditional societies are predominantly ascriptive, diffuse, particularistic, self-oriented, and affective. Modern societies are predominantly achievement oriented, specific, universalistic, collectively oriented, and affectively neutral. The word "predominantly" is an important qualifier, for as Parsons points out, traditional attributes can be observed in the most modern societies, and vice versa.

The anthropologist's delineation of traditional societies is crucial to the political scientist's analysis of development and modernization. "Development," for example, clearly implies progression from one position or stage to another. "Modernization" implies a similar progression from point to point. In both instances, and the words have been used in so many ways that only a general meaning can be discerned; the progression is away from the baseline of traditional societies as defined above and toward social, political economic, and cultural systems organized along the lines of an ideal type of modern society. Although delineations of traditional societies have been adequately supplied by anthropologists, the prototype of the modern society remains a matter of conjecture. Parsons's pattern variables, as well as Weber's rational–legal model and Tonnies's gemeinschaft and gesellschaft, are clearly projections of the more "modern" aspects of behavior and social structure to be found in the most heavily industrialized societies of the world. No existing state can claim to be totally modern, but the United States, Japan, the Soviet Union, and the heavily industrialized states of Western Europe approach and are largely integrated along modern lines. They also appear to be moving in the modern direction. States that remain closely integrated along traditional lines—states generally at the bottom of economic and social development scales—are commonly called underdeveloped. States attempting to move from the traditional toward the modernizing forms of social, economic, and political organization are referred to as developing or modernizing. Generally accepted operationalizations of terms such as development and modernization have yet to be arrived at, but ambitious efforts can be found in David E. Apter's *Some Conceptual Approaches to the Study of Modernization* and in Myron Weiner's *Modernization.*[25] Similarly, a view of the multifarious conceptions of political development can be found in Lucian W. Pye's *Aspects of Political Development.* Pye lists and critiques at least ten definitions, discussing their common elements in the following terms:

The first broadly shared characteristic noted is a general spirit or attitude toward equality. In most views on the subject, political development does involve mass participation and popular involvement in political activities. Participation may be either democratic or a form of totalitarian mobilization, but the key consideration is that subjects should become active citizens, and at least the pretenses of popular rule are necessary. . . .

A second major theme we find in most concepts of political development deals with the capacity of a political system. In a sense, capacity is related to the outputs of a political system and the extent to which the political system can affect the rest of the society and economy. Capacity is also closely associated with governmental performance and the conditions that affect such performance. . . .

A third theme running through much of the discussion of political development is that of differentiation and specialization. This is particularly true in the analysis of institutions and structures. Thus this aspect of development involves first of all the differentiation and specialization of structures. Offices and agencies tend to have their distinct and limited functions, and there is an equivalent of a division of labor within the realm of government.[26]

The anthropologist's delineation of traditional societies and the contrasting typologies of modern and traditional societies do far more for political research than merely establishing the two poles on development scales. They also enable the political scientist to visualize the huge distance between those poles. We know that according to the anthropologists, all facets of life in traditional societies seem to be geared to resist change. From the inculcation of attitudes of passivity, fatalism, and noninnovation through the recruitment of leaders on the basis of ascription and the accentuation of the kinship group as the primary focus of loyalty, the shaping force of traditional society is the preservation of the past. Similarly, the projections of an ideal-type modern society also stress an integrated system of beliefs, structures, and behavior suited to the needs of the rational-ordered, bureaucratic–industrial state. Parsons's pattern variables are opposites: dichotomies between behavior forms in traditional and modern societies. The delineation of polar types and the analysis of the divergent bases of social and political integration located at each extremity, then, enable the political scientist to conceive of the development process, in all its economic, political, and social facets, as far more than a gradual transformation from one social form to another. The development or modernization process features the breakdown or *disintegration* of one form of social life and its associated behavior patterns, and the *reintegration* of the individuals and societies involved into radically new forms of social organization, accompanied by their own demands for radically different behavior patterns. The analysis of the depth of the transition from traditional to modern and the concomitant political problems is the subject of a growing body of political studies, including David E. Apter's *Political Modernization*, Samuel P. Huntington's *Political Order in Changing Societies*, Monte Palmer's *Dilemmas of Political Development*, and Helio Jaguaribe's *Political Development*.[27]

CULTURE

A second area of anthropological research of particular relevance to political scientists centers on the concept of culture and the anthropologist's emphasis on *culture* as the primary determinant in human behavior. As expressed by Margaret Mead:

We are forced to conclude that human nature is almost unbelievably malleable, responding accurately and contrastingly to contrasting cultural conditions. The differences between individuals who are members of different cultures, like the differences between individuals within a culture, are almost entirely to be laid to differences in conditioning, especially during early childhood, and the form of this conditioning is culturally determined.[28]

While emphasizing culture as a major determinant of behavior, anthropologists have experienced serious difficulty in achieving a common, generally accepted conceptual definition of the term. In an attempt to catalog, critically review, and (hopefully) synthesize the common elements contained within major definitions of culture, Kroeber and Kluckholn encountered some 165 different definitions of the concept. In a general sense, they concluded that "Culture is a product, is historical, includes ideas, patterns, and values; is selective; is learned; is based upon symbols; and is an abstraction from behavior and the products of behavior."[29] Another definition is provided by Victor Barnouw:

Here is a definition which I think most anthropologists would accept: A culture is a way of life of a group of people, the configuration of all the more or less stereotyped patterns of learned behavior which are handed down from one generation to the next through the means of language and imitation.[30]

Anthropologists have been understandably cautious in attempting to provide operational definitions of the concept of culture. They are, however, keenly aware that steps in this direction must be taken. The problem is discussed by Albert C. Cafagna:

The recent pronounced interest in the problem of defining the concept "culture" is the most promising sign that cultural anthropology is beginning to emerge from the descriptive phase of its brief scientific career.

Concern over the adequacy of terminology arises when the workers in a particular discipline attempt to formulate general principles, to work out hypotheses, and to arrive at prediction in order to test these hypotheses. Given predefinitional knowledge of culture, ethnographers have reported and described their observations in the field with whatever terms seemed most appropriate for their purposes. As a consequence, what was a "tribe" in one monograph was a "nation" in another, and so on. In order to facilitate communication and to make generalization possible, there arose an effort to adopt standard terms to describe similar phenomena among different peoples. This is the preliminary stage in the development of a scientific terminology. But all that was sought for here was the adoption of standard terms to be used cross-culturally. A certain measure of success has been achieved in this endeavor. But as ethnologists go beyond the mere generalization of facts and attempt to formulate hypotheses to account for these descriptive regularities, their concern with terminology goes beyond that of seeking arbitrary agreement in vocabulary.[31]

In general, then, cultures include the values, norms, and belief systems of a society, including its traditions, customs, religions, ideologies, rituals, heritage, and language, as well as all other shared habits or attributes that might be excluded by these concepts.

Culture, although difficult to define with great precision, has a profound impact on human behavior. Among other things, a culture prescribes values. It tells the individual which physical objects and forms of behavior are important and worthy of preservation and which are to be rejected as worthless or condemned as a threat to society. It sets standards of right and wrong, good and bad, beautiful and ugly. It prescribes norms indicating proper ways for interacting both with members of society and with nonmembers. It distinguishes the "we" from the "they." It establishes the sanctions for disciplining individuals who do not conform to the norms. It provides the individuals with a sense of identity and belonging. It prescribes the individual's rights and obligations. It distinguishes friends from enemies. It affords the individual cathartic outlets by indicating the groups on which he can vent his frustration, thereby alleviating strain and tension within society itself. Furthermore, culture provides a sense of personal security and social solidarity by furnishing individuals with an explanation for their existence, their relationship with the supernatural, and their prospects after death. Finally, culture justifies all the above-named social structures, including existing patterns for the distribution of wealth and power, by making them the will of God, or as in the case of Marxism, the natural, dialectical ordering of the universe.

Culture is the glue that holds societies together. Just as the discussion of roles in Chapter 3 suggested that the concept of role was largely inseparable from the concept of norm (the cultural content of role), the discussion of societies and social structures is inseparable from the concept of culture. Culture, in its broadest sense, is the content of society. It is what individuals living in social structures do and how they behave.

Quite obviously, the more intensely individuals are socialized into their society and shaped by its beliefs and sanctions, the more its content will shape both their overt behavior and their subjective attitudes and ways of viewing their world. Specifically, the more intensely individuals are socialized into their culture, the more stable that society is likely to be, and the greater will be its resistance to change. Recall that the apparent changelessness and stability of traditional societies were due to the content of traditional cultures.

THE POLITICAL RELEVANCE OF CULTURE: POLITICAL CULTURE AND NATIONAL CHARACTER

In our discussion of roles and groups in Chapter 3, we noted the pressures toward conformity that group cultures or subcultures impose on their members. The studies cited indicating the influence of senate norms on the behavior of its members, for example, provide an example of cultural pressures on political behavior. The present discussion, however, is limited to the political influence of total cultures on the political behavior of members of a society. In this regard, two major lines of research have emerged: the study of political culture and the study of national character. The first has developed into a major focus of political research, the second has been largely abandoned by political scientists.

Political Culture
Political culture, as the term suggests, refers to the political scientist's attempt to identify the aspects of culture that are inherently political, particularly the manner in which members of a society perceive or "cognize" political relationships.

The concept, most often associated with Gabriel A. Almond, is best explained in his words.

> . . . The term "political culture" thus refers to the specifically political orientations—attitudes toward the political system and its various parts, and attitudes toward the role of the self in the system. We speak of a political culture just as we can speak of an economic culture or a religious culture. It is a set of orientations toward a special set of social objects and processes. . . .

> We appreciate the fact that anthropologists use the term culture in a variety of ways, and that by bringing it into the conceptual vocabulary of political science we are in danger of importing its ambiguities as well as its advantages. Here we can only stress that we employ the concept of culture in only one of its many meanings: that of *psychological orientation toward social objects*. When we speak of the political culture of a society, we refer to the political system as internalized in the cognitions, feelings, and evaluations of its population. People are inducted into it just as they are socialized into nonpolitical roles and social systems.[32]

In evaluating the level of political culture of a given society, Almond suggests four criteria:

1. What knowledge does he have of his nation and of his political system in general terms, its history, size, location, power, "constitutional" characteristics, and the like? What are his feelings toward these systematic characteristics? What are his more or less considered opinions and judgments of them?
2. What knowledge does he have of the structures and roles, the various political elites, and the policy proposals that are involved in the upward flow of policy making? What are his feelings and opinions about these structures, leaders, and policy proposals?
3. What knowledge does he have of the downward flow of policy enforcement, the structures, individuals, and decisions involved in these processes? What are his feelings and opinions of them?
4. How does he perceive of himself as a member of his political system? What knowledge does he have of his rights, powers, obligations, and of strategies of access to influence? How does he feel about his capabilities? What norms of participation or of performance does he acknowledge and employ in formulating political judgments, or in arriving at opinions?[33]

Based on the above criteria, Almond and Sidney Verba have attempted to delineate three ideal types of *political culture*: parochial, subject, and participant.[34] In the *parochial* culture, typified by the earlier model of traditional societies, the individual is neither directly aware of the operations or policies of the "national political system," nor does he recognize himself as a member of a nation or political system. The parochial individual's horizon, or empathy, is limited to the environs of his tribe or village. He has low physical mobility. He neither understands nor identifies with events beyond his immediate environs. Individuals in "subject political cultures" are described by Almond as follows:

. . . The subject is aware of specialized government authority; he is affectively oriented to it, perhaps taking pride in it; and he evaluates it either as legitimate or as not. But the relationship is toward the system on the general level, and toward the output, administrative or "downward flow" side of the political system; it is essentially a passive relationship.[35]

Participant political cultures, by way of contrast, are those "in which the members of the society tend to be explicitly oriented to the system as a whole and to both the political and administrative structures and processes. . . ." Individuals in participant political cultures are actively involved in the workings of the system. Whether they identify with the system or reject it, they are keenly aware of its influence on their lives, and they seek to influence both the making of policy and the manner in which it is applied.[36]

Almond and Verba also posit three mixed types of political culture: parochial–subject, subject–participant, and parochial–participant. *Parochial–subject* and *subject–participant cultures* are more or less transitional stages between parochial and subject cultures and subject and participant cultures, respectively. In the *parochial–participant culture*, common to many of the developing areas, the political institutions and the values of the leaders are characteristic of a participant political culture, yet the primary loyalties of the masses remain directed toward tribal, village, and religious leaders. Thus although the leaders have created a variety of participant symbols such as flags, constitutions, victory arches, and national anthems, the utility of these symbols in mobilizing the masses or building support for the regime is all but nil.

Almond and Verba thus provide a six-level typology of states based on the "psychic involvement" of the polity. From the perspective of political analysis, the more accurately one can categorize a state, the better able he will be to predict the means elites will use to control and mobilize the masses and the extent to which national leaders will be able to use "symbols" rather than force to persuade the masses to do their bidding. Knowing Nigeria to be a parochial–participant culture, for instance, one should not have been surprised when July 6, 1967 the appeals of Ibo tribal leaders to secede from the Nigerian Federation far outweighed the appeals of the Federation leaders for national unity.

Quite interestingly, Almond and Verba's analysis of the political culture of five democracies (the United States, England, Germany, Italy, and Mexico) led them to conclude that the best cultural climate for a democratic state—a civic culture—was none of the six types listed but, rather, a mixture of several.

The civic culture is a mixed political culture. In it many individuals are active in politics, but there are also many who take the more passive role of subject. More important, even among those performing the active political role of the citizen, the roles of subject and parochial have not been displaced. The participant role has been added to the subject and parochial roles. This means that the active citizen maintains his traditional, nonpolitical ties, as well as his more passive political role as a subject. It is true that the rationality–activist model of the citizen does not imply that participant orientations replace subject and parochial ones; but by not mentioning the latter two roles explicitly, it does not imply that they are irrelevant to the democratic political culture.[37]

Like Parsons's pattern variables, with which it has much in common, Almond's typology of political culture is a useful tool for comparing and contrasting states in differing stages of political development. Like the typologies reviewed earlier, its baseline is a traditional society and its upper limit is a model of projected behavior in an ideal-type modern society based on trends in highly industrialized states. There is also the implicit assumption societies progress from a parochial political culture toward participant political cultures. The assumption is more explicit in Lucian W. Pye's and Sidney Verba's respective articles in their *Political Culture and Political Development.*[38]

Although the concept of political culture has been used primarily in comparative political analysis, Daniel J. Elazer has attempted to employ it in the analysis of American state politics; and more recently Donald J. Devine has applied it to a broad analysis of American government.[39]

National Character

During World War II several anthropologists were drawn into government service, particularly in the Office of War Information.[40] Their main job was to apply the techniques developed in the analysis of primitive cultures to the delineation of "national character" of various opposition and occupied countries. After 1945 the emphasis of character studies shifted to the Soviet Union and Eastern Europe and was augmented by the researchers' ability to make limited visits to the areas of study and by their access to large numbers of Russian and Eastern European emigrés who had defected.

The national character studies were clearly political, but not precisely in the sense of Almond's political culture. Their general assumption was that the more we know about how individuals are shaped by their culture, the greater will be our ability to understand and predict their political behavior. Indeed, this assumption is explicitly stated in Hans J. Morgenthau's *Politics Among Nations*, one of the earliest political science texts to adopt behavioral variables to political analysis, particularly in the field of international relations.

National character cannot fail to influence national power; for those who act for the nation in peace and war, formulate, execute, and support its policies, elect and are elected, mold public opinion, produce and consume—all bear to a greater or lesser degree the imprint of those intellectual and moral qualities which make up the national character. The "elementary force and persistence" of the Russians, the individual initiative and inventiveness of the Americans, the undogmatic common sense of the British, the discipline and thoroughness of the Germans are some of the qualities which will manifest themselves, for better or for worse, in all the individual and collective activities in which the members of a nation may engage. In consequence of the differences in national character, the German and Russian governments, for instance, have been able to embark upon foreign policies that the American and British governments would have been incapable of pursuing, and vice-versa. Antimilitarism, aversion to standing armies and to compulsory military service are permanent traits of the American and British national character. Yet the same institutions and activities have for centuries stood high in the hierarchy of values of Prussia, from where their prestige spread all over Germany. In Russia the traditions of obedience to the authority of the government and the traditional military establishments acceptable to the population.

Thus the national character has given Germany and Russia an initial advantage in the struggle for power, since they could transform in peacetime a greater portion of their national resources into instruments of war. On the other hand, the reluctance of the American and British peoples to consider such a transformation, especially on a large scale and with respect to manpower, except in an obvious national emergency, has imposed a severe handicap on American and British foreign policy. Governments of militaristic nations are able to plan, prepare, and wage war at the moment of their choosing. They can, more particularly, start a preventive war whenever it seems to be most propitious for their cause. Governments of pacifist nations, of which the United States was the outstanding example until the end of the Second World War, are in this respect in a much more difficult situation and have much less freedom of action.[41]

In spite of initial optimism such as that reflected in *Politics Among Nations*, the concept of national character failed to gain acceptance among political scientists. Part of the problem lies in the vagueness of the concept and the difficulty of applying it except in a very general way. A second problem, however, was the unfamiliarity of most political scientists with anthropological techniques and concepts.

CRITIQUE

Perhaps the severist critiques of the concepts primitive and culture have come from anthropologists themselves. As the earlier quotations from Nash and Cafagna indicate, anthropologists are well aware that their major organizing concepts lack definitional clarity—no precise boundaries have been set, and there is no single uniform definition. They also note that without conceptual clarity, operationalization of the concepts of culture and primitive is virtually impossible.

One reason for the lack of systematic concern for conceptual clarity, as Cafagna points out, is simply that "despite their disagreement on how to 'say' what they mean by the word 'culture,' all cultural anthropologists "know" what a cultural trait is when they see one." As long as anthropology remained a primarily descriptive science, greater definitional clarity was not required. As anthropologists have become increasingly concerned with prediction and explanation, they, like political scientists, have been forced to cope with the problems of increased definitional rigor.

Quite clearly, concepts derived from or based on the concepts of *primitive* and *culture* share the definition ambiguity of the parent notions. This is certainly true of the following concepts: *political culture, national character, peasant, traditional, modern, development, developed,* and *modernizing.* The concepts *traditional* and *modern*, used in traditional-modern typologies are really heuristic ideal types. The ideal type "traditional" approximates many characteristics shared by many types of traditional society but glosses over an infinite variety of differences. The ideal type "modern" or "modernity" is further removed from reality in that it is based on projections of the direction in which the world seems to be moving. Furthermore, Parsons's pattern variables are extremely difficult to define conceptually, even given the elaborate efforts at definition in Parsons and Shils's *Toward a General Theory of Action.* "Developing" and "modernizing," imply only a movement from one largely heuristic ideal type to a second heuristic ideal type, and standard usage of the concepts merely implies movement, furnishing little indication of how fast a society must be moving to be considered developing or what the process of development or modernization looks like. This is not to suggest that traditional–modern ideal types and terms such as "developing" and "modernizing" are not useful for visualizing the process of change occurring in much of the world. Vague as the terms themselves are, political scientists recognize examples of development and modernization when they see them. Indeed, given the great lack of empirical information about the process of change and modernization, it may be difficult to formulate more conceptually precise definitions at this time. It is crucial, however, that political scientists remain aware of the ambiguity and imprecision of their concepts and not be lulled into believing them to be more rigorous than they actually are.

The concepts "modern" and "developed" and the concept of "developing" pose other problems as well. All three concepts *imply* a value position. Although often unintended or even specifically denied by authors using the concepts, "modern," "modernizing," and "developing" all imply that "modern" is the ultimate ideal to be attained, that states in the process of the modernization are becoming ideal, and that traditional or undeveloped states, if not bad, are certainly quaint.

The concepts "developing" and "modernizing" also present a teleological problem. Implicit in both is the notion that traditional or underdeveloped states are inexorably moving in the direction of the ideal-type modern society. Some are developing more rapidly than others, but all, it is implied, will eventually make it. Empirical evidence certainly does not support this assumption.

The full range of problems just cited applies to Almond's typology of political cultures. In addition, the concept of political culture suggests that the clearly political aspects of culture can be empirically isolated from the general concept of culture. As anthropological studies have demonstrated, virtually all aspects of culture are political in one form or another. Almond clearly recognized this problem and attempted to avoid it by stressing the individual's psychological perceptions of the political systems. Again, however, perceptions of reality are an artifact of culture in general and are difficult to evaluate without reference to the broader cultural context.

Inherent in the concept of national character, which also shares the general definitional problems associated with the concept of culture, is the methodological error of generalizing from broad cultural traits to individual behavior. The mere existence of traits in a culture does not mean that all individuals associated with that culture possess those traits or that they possess them in equal degrees. The concept of national character also implies that each nation has a particular or distinctive character that persists over time. This assumption clearly ignores the shifts in cultural values that occur over time and in response to changes in environmental circumstances.

Finally, the concept of culture suffers from excessive generality. Few social scientists would quarrel with the anthropologists' contention that culture is a primary determinant of human behavior. However, to say that behavior is influenced by culture is to say that behavior is influenced by values, norms, beliefs, language, traditions, and everything else that gives content to society. In analyzing the shaping of human behavior, anthropological studies must work to delineate specific, rigorously defined, operational concepts within the general rubric of culture. Only in this way can they ascertain which of the various facets of culture are particularly important in the behavior shaping process and how the components thus identified are interrelated.

NOTES

[1] Georges Balandier, *Political Anthropology* (New York: Random House, 1970); Marc J. Swartz, Victor W. Turner, and Arthur Tuden, eds., *Political Anthropology* (Chicago: Aldine, 1966).

[2] Melville J. Herskovits, *Economic Anthropology* (New York: Norton, 1952), see Introduction.

[3] M. Fortes and E. E. Evans-Pritchard, *African Political Systems* (London: Oxford University Press, 1940).

[4] For various aspects of primitive behavior, see: Paul Bohannon, ed., *Law and Warfare* (Garden City, N. Y.: Natural History Press, 1967); Ronald Cohen and John Middleton, eds., *Comparative Political Systems* (Garden City, N.Y.: Natural History Press, 1967); George Dalton, ed., *Economic Development and Social Change* (Garden City, N.Y.: Natural History Press, 1971); George Devereux, *Reality and Dream* (Garden City, N. Y.: Doubleday, 1969).

[5] Manning Nash, *Primitive and Peasant Economic Systems* (San Francisco: Chandler, 1966) p. vii.

[6] Eric R. Wolf, *Peasants* (Englewood Cliffs, N.J.: Prentice-Hall, 1966) pp. 3, 4.

[7] For a review of peasant economic practices, see Nash, *Primitive and Peasant Economic Systems.*

[8] United Nations, *Statistical Yearbook,* 1970.

[9] Nash, *Primitive and Peasant Economic Systems.*

[10] Gideon Sjøberg, "Folk and 'Feudal' Societies," *American Journal of Sociology,* vol. 63, no. 3 (November 1952), p. 231.

[11] David Riesman, *The Lonely Crowd* (New Haven, Conn.: Yale University Press, 1950).

[12] Joseph Lopreato, "Interpersonal Relations in Peasant Society," *Human Organizations*, vol. 21 (Spring 1962), pp. 22–23.

[13] Everett E. Hagen, *On the Theory of Social Change* (Homewood, Ill.: Dorsey, 1962); Talcott Parsons, *Societies* (Englewood Cliffs, N.J.: Prentice-Hall, 1966).

[14] Fortes and Evans-Pritchard, *African Political Systems.*

[15] David E. Apter, *The Gold Coast in Transition* (Princeton, N.J.: Princeton University Press, 1955).

[16] David E. Apter, "The Role of Traditionalism in the Political Modernization of Ghana and Uganda," *World Politics*, vol. 13, no. 1 (October 1960).

[17] D. D. Duncan, ed., *William F. Ogburn on Culture and Social Change* (Chicago: University of Chicago Press, 1964).

[18] Leonard Plotnicov, *Strangers to the City* (Pittsburgh: University of Pittsburg Press, 1967). Oscar Lewis, *Five Families* (New York: Basic Books, 1959).

[19] See: Pitirim A. Sorokin, *Contemporary Sociological Theories* (New York: Harper & Row, 1928); John C. McKinney, *Constructive Typology and Social Theory* (New York: Appleton-Century-Crofts, 1966).

[20] Max Weber, *The Theory of Social and Economic Organization*, trans. by A. M. Henderson and Talcott Parsons (New York: Macmillan, 1947).

[21] Talcott Parsons and Edward A. Shils, eds., *Toward a General Theory of Action* (New York: Harper & Row, 1951).

[22] Ibid.

[23] Henery Habib Ayrout, *The Egyptian Peasant*, trans. John Williams (Boston: Beacon Press, 1962), p. 113.

[24] F. X. Sutton, "Social Theory and Comparative Politics," in Harry Eckstein and David E. Apter, eds., *Comparative Politics* (New York: Free Press, 1963), pp. 67–82.

[25] David E. Apter, *Some Conceptual Approaches to the Study of Modernization* (Englewood Cliffs, N.J.: Prentice-Hall, 1968); Myron Weiner, ed., *Modernization* (New York: Basic Books, 1966).

[26] Lucian W. Pye, *Some Aspects of Political Development* (Boston: Little, Brown, 1966) pp. 45, 47.

[27] David E. Apter, *The Politics of Modernization* (Chicago: University of Chicago Press, 1965); Samuel P. Huntington, *Political Order in Changing Societies* (New Haven, Conn.: Yale University Press, 1968); Monte Palmer, *Dilemmas of Political Development* (Itasca, Ill.: Peacock, 1973); Helio Jaguaribe, *Political Development: A General Theory and a Latin American Case Study* (New York: Harper & Row, 1973).

[28] Margaret Mead, *Sex and Temperament in Three Primitive Societies* (New York: Morrow, 1935).

[29] Alfred Kroeber and Clyde Kluckholn, *Cultures: A Critical Review of Concepts and Definitions* (New York: Random House, Vintage Books, 1952) p. 308.

[30] Victor Barnouw, *Culture and Personality* (Homewood, Ill.: Dorsey, 1963) p. 5.

[31] Albert C. Cafagna, "A Formal Analysis of Definitions of 'Culture'," in Gertrude Dole and Robert L. Carneiro, eds., *Essays in the Science of Culture* (New York: Crowell, 1960) p. 111.

[32] Selections from Gabriel A. Almond and Sidney Verba, *The Civic Culture: Political Attitudes and Democracy in Five Nations* (Copyright © 1963 by Princeton University Press), pp. 13, 14, 16–17, and 474. Reprinted by permission of Princeton University Press.

[33] Ibid.

[34] Ibid., p. 15.

[35] Ibid., pp. 17–18.

[36] Ibid., p. 18.

[37] Ibid., p. 339.

[38] Lucian W. Pye and Sidney Verba, eds., *Political Culture and Political Development* (Princeton, N.J.: Princeton University Press, 1965).

[39] Daniel J. Elazer, *American Federalism* (New York: Crowell, 1966); Donald J. Devine, *The Political Culture of the United States* (Boston: Little, Brown, 1972).

[40] Barnouw, *Culture and Personality*, p. 120.

[41] Hans J. Morgenthau, *Politics Among Nations: The Struggle for Power and Peace*, 5th ed. (Copyright 1948, 1954, © 1960, 1967, 1972, by Alfred A. Knopf, Inc.), pp. 132–133.

5

Economics and Politics

Economics, according to a leading introductory text, is the study of how men and society *choose*, with or without the use of money, to employ *scarce* productive resources to produce various commodities over time and to distribute them for consumption, now and in the future, among people and groups in society.[1]

In pursuing their analyses of the processes of economic choice and distribution, economists have developed a body of concepts and theories that provide a level of predictability far greater than that achieved by most social science disciplines. Indeed, many people consider economics to be the most precise and the most scientific of the social sciences. Regardless of whether this reputation is fully deserved, it must be admitted that economists can "predict and explain" economic behavior much more successfully than political scientists can predict and explain political behavior.

The economist's reputation for greater precision and the ties that have long existed between the disciplines of economics and political science have recently led many political scientists to turn to the economist as a source of helpful ideas in the pursuit of more effective explanation and prediction in politics.

Several concepts and hypotheses developed by economists appear to be directly relevant to the problems of the political scientists. Economists, for instance, have found that assuming that the consumer "behaves rationally" aids in predicting his economic behavior. This being the case, might it not also aid political scientists to assume rationality on the part of voters and government officials? Other concepts such as resource, cost, bargaining, coalition formation, and game theory have similarly offered political scientists valuable perspectives for their analysis of political phenomena. In this chapter, we consider the rational model, then turning to the political insights provided by the concepts resource, cost, bargaining, coalition formation, and game theory.

DECISION MAKING: THE RATIONAL MODEL

Basic to the analysis of economic problems is the decision or choice. Consumers, producers, and traders of both economic and political goods, must make choices among alternatives and decisions concerning actions to be taken. Although decision making is not unique to economic reasoning, the idea of choosing from among alternatives on the basis of their value or utility of the available choices is at the heart of the economic process.

The extent to which decisions can be called rational has been an enduring concern of social research. In economics, the model of rational economic man making rational economic decisions has been very useful. This assumption has been employed in investment forecasting and in the prediction of the choices likely to be made by the consumer. Applications of this idea in political science are becoming more widespread.[2]

Several problems face the researcher who attempts to develop a rational model of political behavior. Among these problems are: (1) lack of an exact, agreed-on definition of "rationality," (2) need to decide whether to treat rationality as an empirical hypothesis or to use it as an assumption in developing a model, and (3) difficulty in articulating and measuring terms that must be used in conjunction with the rationality concept (e.g., the idea of utility and its maximization, as well as terms such as information, risk, and uncertainty[3]).

Rationality in politics involves choosing strategies or alternatives that most efficiently maximize utility (goal achievement) at the least possible cost. Thus a rational governmental decision maker is one who achieves his nation's foreign and domestic goals with the utmost efficiency. Similarly, the rational voter is one who exhaustively collects information about the positions and reliability of various candidates, relates these to his own preferences, and votes accordingly.

Although the concept of the rational voter is appealing, it presents serious obstacles. For one thing, we know that most voters rarely go to the lengths just described in deciding how to vote. The economist Anthony Downs has pointed out that part of the problem stems from the failure of those who build models of the rational voter to properly estimate the cost of information gathering for the typical individual.[4] The cost the average voter faces in trying to collect, sift, evaluate, and absorb potentially relevant information about the candidates soon may lead him to conclude that additional effort would be too much trouble. Downs therefore suggests that on a rational basis very few people in the United States should bother to exert much effort in information gathering.[5] Their costs would probably be greater than the benefits to be gained, since their potential gains are limited by the relatively small differences in the policies of the leading candidates and by the relatively small impact that any single vote is likely to have on the election results. We thus seem to have contradictory interpretations of what constitutes "rational behavior" for the average voter.

Another very interesting contribution in this area is the work of economist Mancur Olson, Jr., dealing with the logic of individual participation in economically oriented interest groups. Discussing the apparent paradox in a labor union, Olson reports: "Over 90 percent will not attend meetings or participate in union affairs; yet over 90 percent will vote to force themselves to belong to the union and make considerable dues payments to it."[6]

By emphasizing a distinction between collective goods such as wage increases, which are received by all members of a group, and other kinds of limited individual rewards, Olson concludes that in a large group, the individuals' "actions and attitudes were a model of rationality when they wished that everyone would attend meetings and failed to attend themselves."[7] This behavior is called rational because the cost of going to the meeting is tangible to the individual, whereas no loss of benefit is likely to result from the absence of any one member of a large organization. The same kind of logic is applicable to the working-class desire for simultaneous tax cuts and increased government services.

It is clear from these examples that the application of

the rationality assumption requires the establishment of consistent standards for deciding whether an individual's behavior is to be classed as rational. Since rationality is defined in terms of efficiently achieving goals or maximizing utilities, the setting of standards boils down to a task of defining and measuring relative utility. This can be done in several ways. One possibility is to infer utility after the fact on the basis of what has been chosen in a given circumstance. Thus we might assume that someone who buys a Cadillac rather than a Volkswagen puts greater value on size, power, and styling than he does on economy and maneuverability. We might also assume that a man who votes for a clearly less qualified candidate of his own party or race puts more value on party or ethnic solidarity than he does on preparation for office. Such an approach, however, merely begs the question. Is it rational to vote for an alcoholic, for example, just because the candidate is a Republican, or a Democrat, or to vote for a man lacking experience or training just because he is black, or white? If the given characteristic of party or race is an important symbol with policy implications, we might conceivably view such behavior as rational. We are likely to be unhappy with the implications of this definition, however, since different individuals may have different identifications. We still must explain why one man votes on ethnic lines and another on party lines. This definition of rationality thus contributes little to our explanation and prediction of actual behavior.

This question can also be approached by having each individual indicate his preference in advance. But even if people are willing to state such preferences, they are often sure in their own minds about many of the choices. When a choice involves a variety of preferences, this approach becomes highly confusing for both the respondent and the researcher. (Chapter 6 deals at some length with the irrational aspects of decision making.)

As a third approach, the researcher can define utility in advance by using criteria external to the decision maker. We may decide that it is in the interest of industrial laborers to vote for a candidate identified as pro labor, or that an executive of an international firm should vote for a candidate who favors free international trade. Such assumptions usually imply a monetary definition of utility. But individuals are legitimately concerned about things other than money— personal safety, for example. Thus utility is best defined on the basis of the relative importance to each individual of these and other goals, depending on the personal circumstance of each chooser. When rigid standards of rationality are applied, however, most individuals are so irrational that a rational model becomes inappropriate.

Why are political decisions prone to irrationality? Discounting personality factors to be discussed in Chapter 6, the information factor alone mitigates against the making of rational decisions. A decision is not likely to be completely rational with respect to the achievement of previously defined goals unless the individual has perfect information about the impact of each of his potential actions on each of his goals. He should also have a good estimate of the utility associated with each outcome and of the costs of such decisions. The problem is obvious. Perfect information, or even anything closely approximating it, is rarely found in an actual decision situation. Many individuals make consistently rational choices in tightly controlled experimental situations, but it is a long way from the perfect information of the laboratory, or even the relatively high level of information in the marketplace, to the chaos of the political arena.

Also, most decisions are made in a state of partial uncertainty about outcomes. We do not always know whether we will like a particular movie before we have seen it. We are not sure we will approve of a governor's actions until he has been in office for a while. In fact, all the alternatives available to an individual may not be known. Most people, for example, are not fully aware of their rights to information about the governmental process. Free documents published by national and state governments, which are available to all voters, are only ordered and read by a handful of political activists. Many people do not know that this information is available. Particularly in the case in primary elections, voters do not know the names of all the candidates or their backgrounds. This lack of complete information introduces an element of risk into such decisions, making the rational model more difficult to apply.

An additional problem faced by proponents of a rational

model is the difficulty of combining the utilities of individuals into a single measure of social utility, thus allowing for rational decision making at the group or the national level. When each individual has only two choices, we can simply add up the votes.[8] We then know which of the two alternatives is preferred by the majority. This solves the problem of social utility if we assume that preferences of every individual are equally strong or that differences in such strengths of preference are irrelevant or unimportant. If several alternatives are available, however, we have no adequate solution.[9] Since different individuals may rank three or more alternatives in any order, there may be no clear preference for any one of the choices.

The principle can also be seen in government decisions about the relative importance of national security, economic growth, and individual liberty. Suppose that one-third of the people rank growth first, security second, and liberty third. A second group of equal size rank security first, liberty second, and growth third. The remainder rank liberty first, growth second, and security third. Obviously there is no clear rule for deciding which of the three goals should have the highest priority. We can also demonstrate readily that no such rule can be established as long as no one of the three groups attains over 50 percent of the total.

If more than three issues or alternatives are involved, the probability of obtaining a solution becomes proportionately lower.

If only two candidates have run for an office, we knew from the ballot count which one is preferred by a majority of voters. If four candidates run, however, a majority might prefer the third-place finisher to the one who finished first, if they had to choose between only these two! Kenneth Arrow, who has devoted considerable attention to this problem, concludes that except under quite limited conditions, it is probably impossible to combine individual utility and a social utility function.[10] James S. Coleman, in reviewing this issue, suggests that an essential element in such situations is the recognition that decision making takes place under conditions of uncertainty and that individuals' intensities of preference must also be considered.[11] Trade-offs are thus allowed, and a variety of items are considered in tandem. One such issue may be the decision-making process itself. Individuals may prefer a slightly less rewarding decision outcome, for instance, when the choice is made by a preferred process. Particular democratic values (or consensus on other rules for decision making) thus may be widely shared and may become a part of individual utility considerations.[12] In this way, perhaps, a connection between individual preferences and social choice can be made, at least for the duration of consensus on the processes of decision making in the group, community, or political system. These problems have led some scholars, perhaps prematurely, to plead that rational models be discarded in favor of models of nonrationality or even irrationality.[13] Nevertheless, several investigators have found limited rationality assumptions to be valuable in interpreting political behavior. Riker and Zavoina, using evidence from an experimental situation constructed to investigate the decision process of politicians, concluded that the assumption of rational utility maximization fit the evidence better than alternative models.[14]

Similarly, Arthur Goldberg discovered that deviations of American children from the party identification of the parents are most common among those with high educational attainment and occur most frequently when the father's party identification does not fit the social and economic position of the next generation's family.[15] Such deviations are least common among those with high educational attainment when fathers' identifications do fit the children's socio-economic level. The implication is clearly that education reduces cost of information, thus increasing "objective" rationality. This principle is most applicable when the decision maker has reliable information. Thus if a political candidate has information concerning voter preferences for federal aid to education or federal grants to cities, and he makes related programs prominent in his campaign platform we might say that he has acted rationally.

In summary, the successful application of the rationality assumption requires considerable care in the definition of key terms. Serious difficulties are to be expected in highly complex situations. Nevertheless, rationality has some promise of helping us to organize our understanding of certain kinds of political phenomena, although it also is unlikely to provide a model for predicting and explaining the entirety of politics.

RESOURCES

Although entire models drawn from economics have limited value as models for political analysis, several individual concepts have been very helpful to the political scientist. One of these is the idea of resources—that is, the notion of anything that can be used by an individual, group, or nation in the pursuit of its goals.[16] These may be spent or used up, such as money or military equipment. They may be exchanged for other goods, as when groups or individuals bargain to exchange support in issue areas of special importance to each party. Thus a Florida congressman may promise to support farm subsidies if a fellow congressman from Iowa will support federal aid to the elderly. Alternatively, resources may be invested to achieve outcomes that would in turn increase the original stock of resources. An aspiring politician may devote hours of study to the law or to learning the names of key people in a congressional district. Or he may devote his energies to the nitty-gritty of volunteer campaign work for others in the hopes of improving his chances in a future campaign for higher office.

Resources can also be thought of as constraints. A man may wish to spend time with his wife and family and may also be somewhat interested in supporting the candidacy of a particular person for sheriff, mayor, or the legislature. If he is not able to devote as many resources to both his family and the campaign as he would like, it becomes necessary for him to allocate his resources between the two choices. He must compare the benefits to be obtained by passing out campaign literature with the cost of time, money, and resources incurred. He must also consider the benefits given up by choosing to spend less time with his family. For some people the same kind of problem is involved in the simple choice of whether to even cast a ballot. Since it is often possible to measure such resources as time and money, a focus on resources helps us to understand related decisions more clearly and to explain and predict them more effectively.

The variety of political resources is almost limitless. Time, money, and votes are obvious resources. Robert A. Dahl, in his study of New Haven, Connecticut, has shown the importance of social standing as a resource in community decision making.[17] Yet other resources range from control over jobs and information to charisma or popularity.

In some areas of the world, the severe inequality of land ownership makes land a crucial political resource. The landowner's control over peasant jobs often leaves the peasant little option but to support the political choices of his landed "patrón." This situation has been particularly important in Latin America and is only slowly changing.[18]

Political protest may also be viewed as a political resource, although not always an effective one. Michael Lipsky has suggested that protest is most often used by groups that have numbers but lack status, contacts, and a ideology that fits the majority view.[19] Such groups have few other resources that offer any hope of success. Concentration on resources thus helps us to place protest in perspective, since we are led to recognize how few alternative resources and options are available to most groups.

At the international level, resources are essential in the determination of national power and capabilities.[20] What a nation such as the United States can accomplish is heavily dependent on its sources of supply for energy, manpower, and other resources. These factors involve the process of resource mobilization and allocation. Where government ownership and regulation is extensive, capabilities should be high, since they can be channeled according to a plan by a central authority. Production may be low, however, if performance incentives have not been provided to key elements of the population. National power (see Chapter 2 on the use of power) includes not only mineral resources, area, population, and military equipment, but also motivational elements such as national cohesion and popular support for government initiative. Similarly, population is a resource, but it will be difficult to achieve key goals if the people are not adequately trained and placed. Land, mineral resources, and hard currency for international exchange are important resources, but unless they are effectively concentrated in the hands of individuals with consistent principles and goals, goal achievement will be very difficult. Thus a government's planning and administrative capacity should also be thought of as political resources.

It is not always easy to convert resources into influence over policy outcomes. For example, it is probably very difficult for political candidates to convert social status and large finances into popularity except insofar as a minimum amount of such resources is necessary for the candidate to be recognized by the voters.[21] In fact, an opponent with slender resources can sometimes turn an opponent's more favorable situation into an advantage for himself. In the North Carolina gubernatorial campaign of 1972, the large expenditures by Democratic candidate Hargrove Bowles were effectively exploited by his Republican opponent in a television spot that featured a pile of dollar bills. Similarly, in spite of its overwhelming resource superiority, the United States was unable to achieve its announced goals in South Vietnam.

Time preferences in the achievement of goals are also important in decisions concerning the use of resources. Some resources increase in value with use, others depreciate. This factor must be considered in such diverse cases as a legislator's decision on how to vote on a tax bill; a citizen's decision whether to campaign actively for a given candidate, to make financial contributions, or to do nothing; or a national policy maker's decision regarding initiatives to be taken in Southeast Asia or the Middle East, and when to make them. It may be impossible to accomplish goals without a certain minimum amount of resources, and lesser amounts may be wasted. This is particularly true concerning the production of collective goods. It would be silly to spend enough money to build half a rocket to the moon or one-third of a nuclear submarine. If resources are not available for a complete unit, it is better to wait until they can at least be anticipated.

Dealing with resources helps us to see such problems in perspective, reminding us that no one, including the President, has unlimited resources. It also helps us to determine what resources we have and where they can most effectively be used for short- and long-term accomplishment of political and social goals.

EXCHANGES

Resources have an effect in the marketplace when they are exchanged for another good. Discussion of exchanges in the political realm are found in writings of philosophers and economists from Plato and Aristotle to Locke, Smith, Bentham, and Malthus.[22] Contemporary applications of economic reasoning to political analysis have attempted to formalize these discussions and to clarify the assumptions involved.[23]

In economic terms, an *exchange* is a situation in which each of two parties provides a certain quantity of goods and receives other goods from the other party. In political terms, financial contributions, votes, or other kinds of resource may be usable as goods for such an exchange. Kochen and Deutsch have suggested a typology consisting of three currencies that may be used in political exchanges.[24] These include positional currencies, decisional currencies, and material currencies. The appointment of leaders and the definition of the responsibilities and scope of authority to be assigned to a given officer are political resources of the positional type. The controversy between advocates of the government hiring practices referred to as "spoils system" and the merit system indicates the importance of this kind of currency.

Decisional currencies involve such questions as who shall participate in the decision process and what weight each participant will carry. The debate over the extension of the vote to 18-year-olds or compromises such as the one that led to equal representation of states in the United States Senate are examples of this kind of currency.

Finally, material currencies are those we most commonly think of as currencies. Government funds, collected by taxes or other revenue sources; government services, such as police protection; or government-produced goods, such as electricity from government-operated dams, are all examples of material political currencies. Also worthy of mention is government credit extended through special loans for students, farmers, homeowners, and veterans. The rules regulating the availability of such services have an obvious political character and can be usefully viewed in terms of political exchanges.

How are such exchanges regulated? Dahl and Lindblom have suggested a four-way classification of regulating mechanisms including voting, market choice, delegation, and autonomous social choice.[25] Each method of regulation must be evaluated on the basis of its capacity (1) to provide clear and unique answers to problems of exchange regulation, and (2) to achieve and maintain legitimacy for the decision-making process. When alternatives can be formulated as a "yes" or "no" choice, voting is often the relevant mode for deciding on such exchanges. A decision to accept or reject a new health program, for example, is much easier to deal with than a decision phrased in terms of alternative plans. Voting is seldom difficult to legitimize, although at times different rules requiring special majorities are established as prerequisites for initiating new exchange types or exchanges of specific kinds.

As a method of regulating exchanges, market choice is commonly accepted when economic goods are concerned, but it carries less legitimacy with respect to the political process. The major problems associated with this method are the difficulty in limiting the number of alternatives and the need to define equivalent values for various political goods in terms of a common currency. There is no obvious equivalent for money in political science. Nevertheless, certain kinds of government decision, particularly with respect to allocation of financial goods, are influenced by market choice. The decision to administer the postal service as a special agency, not as a department headed by a cabinet official, is an example of a governmental effort to improve efficiency by allowing greater market influences on its handling of some of its services.

The third method, delegation, involves the regulation of exchanges by a single individual or a small group of individuals chosen from the community at large. Delegation may thus consist of regulation by elected officials, regulation by officials chosen by the rules of an earlier exchange, or, in its extreme form, coercion by a totalitarian leadership.

Our final method of regulating exchange is autonomous social choice. Here each individual adjusts his goals until they fit those of the rest of the community. This is what happens when people who have previously cut across a green decide to take one path to avoid tearing up the whole lawn. Autonomous social choice is probably less important than the other methods in analyzing political decision making, particularly in formal terms.

Economists have tended to emphasize the importance of market choice as a regulating mechanism, whereas political scientists generally favor voting and delegation. All these approaches have applications in both political and economic analyses. A focus on exchange helps to explain the political process by directing attention to precisely what is being exchanged between what parties, and what kinds of currencies are being used. Thus we may recognize otherwise neglected but important aspects of the political process.

COSTS

The previous discussion indicates the importance of costs in the decision-making process. There are various kinds of cost, both for the individual and for society. Any decision involves estimates of both resource costs and opportunity costs. Opportunity costs refer to what might have been accomplished if alternative goals or means had been chosen.

Of particular importance in individual political decision making are participant costs and what might be called subjective indirect costs.[26] Any individual who participates actively in the political process is sacrificing resources that could be used in achieving other, nonpolitical goals. These costs include time he spends in such activity, the value of his labor, and the costs of obtaining information about the problem on which action is taken.

Opportunity costs must also be considered against the probable rewards that will be obtained as a result of a particular set of actions. Subjective indirect costs are involved in deciding whether an action is to be taken. Thus fear of possible personal consequences or cynicism about the potential for change may inhibit action. Apathy may have a similar effect.

Costs are also relevant in dealing with the choice of tactics. The way an individual perceives his costs may be related to the numbers of individuals involved in a given action, the probable costs to each individual usually decreasing with an increase in the size of the group. If 20 students are involved in a protest, all could conceivably be suspended. If 3000 students participated, a university could not afford to expel them all, or even most of them.

Costs are entailed in government decision making in at least two ways: (1) the costs of the decision-making process, its organization, and efficiency, and (2) the costs of actual policy outcomes to the individuals who are directly affected by that policy. Dahl and Lindblom have discussed several potential costs of the organization of decision making, particularly the costs involved in the development of a hierarchy.[27] Such costs include "red tape" or the proliferation of sometimes unnecessary rules and regulations, reluctance to make decisions that might focus personal responsibility for error, rigidity and inflexibility that may be produced by the desire to maintain one's position, or by a combination of strong identification with the agency or department and intense specialization on the part of the employees. Other costs are impersonality (although necessary, it is nevertheless a cost for the achievement of many types of goal) and excessive centralization, which is perhaps a natural response to some of the other problems.

Another issue arises when individuals within a community are taxed because of budget and appropriations decisions made by government authorities. These costs are distributed through tax law and through such legislation as that establishing the Federal Housing Administration. When recognized, these costs may stimulate those bearing the heaviest burdens to action. This is especially likely to happen when the cost of present policy to the taxpayers is perceived by them as exceeding the cost of their participant efforts plus the costs of an alternative that might be achieved as a result of such participation.

Some costs, particularly opportunity costs, are difficult to measure. However, estimates of cost are such a significant aspect of choice that every effort must be made to consider all important costs to be able to predict the success of outcomes and, in politics, the feedback that can be expected from interested parties at all levels.[28]

BARGAINING

Exchanges between individuals sometimes do not take place immediately, even when both sides desire to make an exchange. Sometimes the parties feel that an agreement can be worked out, but mutually acceptable terms are not yet obvious. In such cases bargaining takes place. Bargaining is the attempt to arrive at mutually acceptable terms for the exchange of goods through the exchange of information about the goal priorities of each party and about the relative values of the goods to be exchanged.[29] Such information exchanges must normally be limited to a small number of individuals, who may act either for themselves or as representatives for larger groups. Dahl and Lindblom suggest that bargaining is best viewed as a form of reciprocal control among leaders.[30] In the economic arena, collective bargaining between unions and management follows this pattern. In the political system, exchanges of this type are quite common among popularly elected representatives, among interest group representatives, and between both these groups and members of the bureaucracy. The relationships between interest groups, such as the AFL–CIO or the National Association of Broadcasters, and government regulatory agencies, such as the National Labor Relations Board or the Federal Communications Commission, can be viewed in terms of reciprocal control. Relations between the President and congressional leaders, especially those of the opposite party, can be examined in these terms as well.

Bargaining is possible when each of two actors, delegates, or representatives values goods held by the other more than he values those which he himself holds. If this imbalance is obvious, an exchange may take place without bargaining. Terms of exchange are important, however, in setting precedents for future exchanges. Thus such a quick exchange seldom occurs unless social norms or the market process have specified a reasonable exchange between the two types of goods. In the political sphere, the difficulty of measuring values of goods has meant that a clear, stable exchange rate is usually unavailable. Thus bargaining is needed on almost every issue to arrive at terms of exchange that are at least provisionally acceptable to all.

Perhaps the most systematic discussion of bargaining is found in the writings of Thomas C. Schelling. In *The Strategy of Conflict*, Schelling discusses the structure of the negotiation process, as well as the importance of the promise, the threat, and bluff. He begins his discussion with the following paradoxical statement:

. . . The power to constrain an adversary may depend on the power to bind oneself; . . . in bargaining, weakness is often strength, freedom may be freedom to capitulate, and to burn bridges behind one may suffice to undo an opponent.[31]

A key to successful bargaining is the ability to convince the other party of the rigidity of your position. In buying a house, the best deal is made by the person who can commit himself irrevocably to a price that is just barely preferable (to the seller) than no sale at all. The same is true for bargaining between interest groups or between nations. Thus it may be advantageous to an American President engaged in trade negotiations with Europe, Japan, or the Soviet Union to have all parties know that he is limited by the need for congressional approval of the offers he can make to a potential trading partner. This will be especially true if it is known that some kind of trade agreement is considered highly desirable.

Schelling goes on to discuss a variety of bargaining situations. Regarding tacit bargaining, in which communications are incomplete or impossible, Schelling finds that it makes little difference whether the same outcome is desired by both parties. In many cases, an obvious solution is agreed on. He reports:

Among all the available options, some particular one usually seems to be the focal point for coordinated choice, and the party to whom it is a relatively unfavorable choice quite often takes it simply because he knows that the other will expect him to.[32]

This, of course, will be true only if the solution, although relatively unfavorable to one of the bargainers, appears better to both sides that does no bargain at all.

Wade and Curry identify the following, four types of actors involved in the political bargaining process: beneficiaries, fiduciaries, politicians, and spectators.[33] The *beneficiary* is the actor who, as a member of one or more groups, receives benefits as a result of political bargains achieved. He normally will pay the costs of membership dues in a group to enable himself to take advantage of the bargaining power of the group. A member of a labor union or a manufacturer of defense equipment might be beneficiaries under this definition.

The *fiduciary* represents the group as its agent. He is responsible for bargaining with other groups on issues in which his group has an interest, and he tries to influence government allocation of resources in a manner favorable to the group he represents. He receives a return from the group for his services in the bargaining process, usually in the form of a salary. An interest group lobbyist or a labor negotiator are fiduciaries, as the word is used here.

The *spectator* is not a member of any group, perhaps due to lack of interest in the issues, or, alternatively, because the costs of membership appear to be greater than the value he could expect to gain through membership. In political terms, however, the spectator may be involved in the election process and may be subject to external costs, such as taxes; he may also receive external rewards. A nonunion worker in an open shop who receives the benefits of a wage increase negotiated by the union is a "spectator" receiving an external reward.

The *politician* participates directly in the allocation of rewards and costs for the whole society. In return for his time, energy, and expenses of office, he receives power, prestige, and deference, as well as salary, expense money, and contributions. He must deal with the electorate, mostly made up of spectators, and with the fiduciaries of groups.

Since time and effort spent in the bargaining process must be viewed as a cost, two people are not likely to engage in bargaining unless both feel that acceptable terms of exchange can be reached. However, since the purpose of bargaining is to achieve the best terms of exchange for your side, strategy is used to affect the bargaining conditions by changing the other side's perception of your own preferences. Thus you try to convince him that your goods are worth more to both of you than is actually the case, and that his goods are worth less.[34] In negotiating a coalition between organized labor and blacks, for example, each side would try to place its own high-priority goals on the common list by arguing that its resources will make the greater contribution to the common venture and that perhaps one could achieve its own goals just as effectively without forming the coalition.

Of course, the degree to which each side can exaggerate is limited by the desire to bargain well in the future. Such qualities as credibility are important components of the ability to reach successful bargains. The *promise* is a major bargaining tool; it is even a potential element of exchange. But it is only effective if it is believable to the other party. *Threats*, the other side of the same coin, have their value in the implication that the threat will not be carried out if an exchange takes place on the threatener's terms. Both the promise and the threat are dependent on credibility, whether in a congressional debate or in international treaty negotiations over arms control and the proliferation of nuclear weapons.[35]

COALITIONS

The terms that are likely to result from bargaining between groups and their representatives are largely dependent on the bargaining power held by each party. Bargaining power is made up of available resources, alternative sources of supply for the desired goods, and the skill and credibility of the bargainers. The weaker side of such a bargain may, of course, seek to form a coalition with a third party to improve his bargaining position. This should increase the probability that he will be able to achieve better terms for himself, but it also will mean that he must share the returns obtained by the coalition with his partners.

Coalitions are generally more highly prized by the weaker member of the coalition, who usually receives a greater proportionate share than the stronger member, if the difference in their respective bargaining powers is significant. This is because the stronger coalition partner makes side payments to the weaker member in exchange for the latter's support. The experience of German political parties in the postwar period is a good example of this. Both the small Free Democratic Party and the Christian Social Union have received more than their proportionate share of cabinet posts in coalition governments in which they have participated.

The American two-party system can be viewed as a pair of coalitions created to achieve given goals through such competitions as the election of the President, or through the organization of Congress. This perspective helps us understand the continuous bargaining process between liberals and conservatives in both parties. It also provides one potential explanation of why Southerners hold more than their share of congressional leadership posts. Southerners form the weaker but still essential coalition partner within the coalition that is the Democratic party. Thus we should not be surprised to see them holding numerous posts as long as they maintain a certain level of cohesion with respect to congressional decision making.

The importance of coalition formation and the bargaining process can be even more clearly seen in European systems, such as Germany, Italy, or the French Fourth Republic. Here the absence of a majority party has usually required that two or more parties participate in the division of cabinet posts to achieve a majority of pro-government delegates in the national legislature. The time-honored process of log-rolling in the American Congress is another example of bargaining among individuals to form a successful coalition, although coalitions thus formed are usually short-lived.

William H. Riker has carefully studied the question of the optimal size of coalitions. He suggests that under ideal circumstances, individuals or groups will try to form coalitions just large enough to win a desired goal, allowing them to share the fruits of victory with the smallest possible number of people. Thus a political party in a presidential system would be expected to level off in size when it has enrolled slightly more than 50 percent of the electorate, building an additional margin only large enough to take care of uncertainty. When special majorities are required for specific kinds of change, a party may have to strive for a higher percentage of the goal. Thus if a two-thirds majority is required to obtain action, a coalition will try to add to its membership until this figure is reached. If unanimity is required, consensus is attempted, and whatever bargaining takes place is done within the group.

The greater the level of consensus within the group, the greater the possibility of achieving the special majorities required. But when broad consensus already exists, there is less demand for such majorities. Thus the United States, which is probably somewhat less homogeneous than Britain, has more rules requiring special majorities but more difficulty in achieving such conditions. Since the filibuster, our machinery for making constitutional amendments, and the presidential veto can all be viewed as situations featuring special majorities, it is clear that bargaining within coalitions is of great importance in the American political process.

In addition to providing intuitive insights into political phenomena, economic bargaining has direct relevance for the political process. Consider the role of government in facilitating bargaining between labor and employers—that is, as supplier of information concerning the preference of spectators in the process, to forestall the need for them to pay exorbitant external costs as a result of the bargain achieved. Such costs, if permitted, might lead to a breakdown in the established bargain between these spectators and the incumbent politicians. In other words, the latter might be voted out of office in the next election. This role of government is often described as the protection of the "national interest," a concept that is very difficult to define. An important and increasing task is entailed, however, and for government to abandon this role would precipitate the breakdown of market control over wages, prices, and conditions of employment, which can occur when extensive and powerful coalitions are formed by both workers and employers, as in modern society.

THE THEORY OF GAMES

Attempts to quantitatively manipulate economic concepts such as bargaining, coalition formation, and competition have led to the introduction of mathematical game theory into social science research. Game theory is the first area of mathematics whose development was inspired primarily by social science problems. As a result, it probably offers a greater potential for the interpretation of social and political problems than do other branches of mathematics.[36]

Game theory consists of the formal analysis of relationships between or among actors; each actor has a specified number of alternative actions or strategies in a given situation, and the results for each actor are dependent on the decisions or strategies chosen by the other actors. It is assumed that each actor is attempting to maximize his payoff (goal achievement or reward) as a result of participating in the "game." It is also assumed that each player will engage in a rational calculation of his expected outcomes, choosing the strategy most favorable to himself.

Game theoretical analysis requires the construction of a game theoretic matrix,[37] in which the pay-offs satisfy at least the assumption of an ordinal scale. In other words, we can say that any outcome that might be obtained by any actor has a value to him that is either greater than, equal to, or less than the value to him of any other possible outcome. Suppose, for example, that a Republican congressman is obliged to vote for a bill that is sponsored by a Republican President but opposed by the congressman's constituents. He has four outcomes, which can be ranked as follows: (1) vote with the President and win, (2) vote with the constituency and win, (3) vote with the constituency and lose, (4) vote with the President and lose. He will obviously be advised to vote with the President if he thinks the bill will pass and with the constituency if he thinks it will fail. Game theory accomplishes the generalization of this simple kind of advice to other kinds of decision.

Games are classified into types based on a set of criteria concerning the rules of the game. The most common distinction is between the two-person game and the *n*-person game, where *n* is any number of players greater than 2. Also of great importance is the difference between zero-sum games and variable-sum games.[38] In a zero-sum or constant-sum game, any advantage gained by one participant must be balanced by an equivalent loss by one or more other participants. In a variable-sum game, it is possible for both players to win or for both players to lose at the same time, although one of the participants would normally win or lose more or less than the other(s); i.e., gains or losses would not necessarily be equal.

Also important in distinguishing among types of games is knowledge of whether information can be exchanged among players before they choose their strategies, thus allowing bargaining about the choices to occur. The distinction between games that do and do not allow side payments can be useful, too. Side payments represent attempts to induce others to follow a strategy favorable to you by offering the others part of your pay-off in exchange for their assistance.

The most advanced theoretical developments in game theory have been in the analysis of two-person, zero-sum games, which are directly applicable to political problems only when a state of pure competition exists between two individuals, two states, or two rigidly defined alliances.

Most political situations, however, are not straight win-or-lose propositions. For example, in analyzing the relationship between the United States and the Soviet Union, which share certain goals, a nonzero or variable-sum game is clearly a more appropriate model. In *Conflict and Defense*, Kenneth Boulding outlines five basic types of game theoretical model that can be used in different cases.[39]

The Pure Conflict Model   This is the basic two-person, zero-sum game, in which a gain for one side means an equivalent loss for the other side. As illustrated by Equation 5.1, every possible outcome contains both a winner and a loser. The first number in each cell represents an estimate of the utility of that option to the United States. The second number in each cell represents the estimated utility of that option to the Soviet Union. Thus the upper left-hand cell of Equation 5.1 represents a loss (−1) for the United States and a win (1) for the Soviet Union.

$$\text{USSR}$$

(5.1)   United States $\begin{cases} -1,1 & 2,-2 \\ -2,2 & 1,-1 \end{cases}$

The Mixed-Conflict, Symmetrical Game   The disarmament problem may be an example of this type of game. Let us suppose that both the United States and the Soviet Union favor disarmament, but only if the other side will disarm also. The pay-off matrix may resemble Equation 5.2.

$$\text{USSR}$$

(5.2)   United States $\begin{array}{l} \text{Disarm} \\ \text{Not disarm} \end{array} \begin{cases} +10,+10 & -100,+50 \\ +50,-100 & -50,-50 \end{cases}$

This formation illustrates a particular insight of game theory and is known as the Prisoner's Dilemma, because it is analogous to the problem of two prisoners, each of whom has been offered leniency if he will testify against the other prisoner before the other agrees to testify against him.[40] If neither agrees, both will be prosecuted for a lesser charge. If both testify, both will be convicted. But if only one testifies, he will receive a suspended sentence while the other receives a very stiff sentence. If the two cannot trust each other, both will probably testify to avoid the stiffest personal sentence, although each could do better if neither were to testify.

We can see from the matrix that both countries would prefer to have both sides disarm rather than continue the arms race, which is a drain on both economies. But unless they can communicate their preference to each other in advance, *and* unless each can be confident that he can trust the other to honor an agreement to disarm (strategy 1), each will continue to increase his arms stockpile. This is true because this strategy (strategy 2) is more advantageous to each one *no matter which strategy the other chooses, if neither knows in advance what the other will do.* Thus they arrive at a result that both find worse than mutual disarmament.

Mixed Conflict, Asymmetrical   In this situation the two parties are of vastly unequal size or resources, the pay-off matrix resembling Equation 5.3.

$$\text{(5.3)} \quad \text{Country B} \begin{array}{c} \text{Country A} \\ \text{Disarm} \quad \text{Arm} \\ \begin{array}{l} \text{Disarm} \\ \text{Arm} \end{array} \begin{Bmatrix} 9,1 & 8,0 \\ 7,2 & 8,-1 \end{Bmatrix} \end{array}$$

The result is a circular pattern, where country B arms first, moving from (9, 1) to (7, 2). This encourages A to arm, thus moving to (8, −1). Now B is encouraged to disarm, moving to (8, 0). Finally A can gain one unit by disarming, and the circle is ready to begin again.

Here it is implied that in relations between highly unequal and potentially hostile states or alliances, a cycle of arming and disarming initiated by the weaker side will appear rational to both if values associated with each possible arrangement are ordered in a certain manner.

Pure Cooperation   In this situation one solution is best for both parties, and all intermediate stages lead in the direction of that solution. A matrix like Equation 5.4 would produce that result.

$$\text{(5.4)} \quad \begin{Bmatrix} 1,1 & 0,0 \\ 0,0 & -1,-1 \end{Bmatrix}$$

It should be noted that any such cooperative model must be a variable-sum game rather than a zero-sum game.

Mixed Cooperation   When any move will increase the total pay-off to both participants, but not necessarily to each, and a side payment from the more fortunate participant may transform the game into one of the pure cooperation type (Eq. 5.4), we have mixed cooperation. In the game in Equation 5.5,

$$\text{(5.5)} \qquad\qquad \overset{\displaystyle A}{B \begin{Bmatrix} 2,0 & -1,2 \\ 1,3 & 0,0 \end{Bmatrix}}$$

both players will want to achieve a total outcome of (1, 3) but only if there is a side payment from B to A to induce A to move from (2, 0). Alternatively, a side payment from A to B may earlier have been made to force a move from (−1, 2) to (2, 0).

The foregoing discussion assumes that a *minimax* strategy has been adopted by the participants. In simple terms, this means that each will try to make his choices to minimize the possible loss to himself, regardless of the choices of the other participant. These examples also involve two-person games. When more than two persons "play," the situation becomes more complex.

The use of game theory in an *n*-person situation is illustrated by the analysis of democratic choice by Buchanan and Tullock, in which they show that a majority voting system may lead to an irrational result of public investment in less reproductive public works.[41] This may be the case featuring a significant difference in the net return of the various projects proposed by individual representatives. The somewhat complex reasoning is based on showing that supporters of less efficient projects will be more numerous than supporters of the most efficient project and that the former will often lack incentives to support the most efficient project rather than and will be more likely to form a majority coalition with proponents of other less efficient projects. The authors also discuss the possibility of an overconcentration of resources in public projects, due to the pure, simple-majority voting system.[42]

The analysis of rationality was clarified when it was discovered in the analysis of *n*-person games that in situations involving more than two actors, two kinds of rationality emerge which are not always consistent with each other— that is, a rationality related to each actor operating independently, and a rationality of all actors acting collectively. Collective action can only be more rational than individual rationality if there is trust that everyone will play fair. This has already been mentioned in our discussion of the Prisoner's Dilemma. In Equation 5.1, for instance, it is quite obvious that the total pay-off for the United States and the USSR in disarming is $+2$, whereas the total value to both sides of all other outcomes is less than zero. Yet a pure strategy for each individual actor leads to solutions other than the one that is collectively "best." The same analysis can be applied to "pork barreling" among sponsors of inefficient projects. The analysis of such games indicates that the introduction of side payments allows for the congruence of individual and collective rationality in some circumstances.[43] Game theory is also useful in the analysis of coalition formation. Riker has used game theory to predict that the coalitions that are formed will consist of the minimum number of members necessary to achieve a desired goal. In an analysis of the 1824 presidential election, he uses this principle to explain the coalition between John Q. Adams and Henry Clay which led to the election of Adams, although he did not have a plurality of the vote.[44]

Other efforts in game theory have involved the application of tree diagrams for the analysis of a series of decisions to be made in sequence or for the analysis of more complex conditional strategies.[45] Discussion of more complex games, however, exceeds the scope of this book.

In summary, game theory is an abstract, deductive, mathematical formulation for the analysis of relationships among individuals and collective actors, such as groups, parties, and nations. Different game types are appropriate for the analysis of conflict, cooperation, bargaining, and coalition formation. In the application of game theory, we confront (1) the difficulty in filling in the values of the pay-off matrix, a step that is essential if we are to determine rational strategies for playing the game; (2) the difficulty in determining unique solutions to several classes of game, leaving the analyst with several possible interpretations rather than just one; and (3) the high level of abstraction of the theory, which often complicates direct application to specific political and social problems. Game theory has been extremely helpful in suggesting and ferreting out certain inconsistencies in our interpretation of rational strategy. It has also contributed new perspectives for the analysis of bargaining and decision and has been valuable as well in clarifying our understanding of such terms as utility, rationality, and coalitions.

SPATIAL MODELING

An additional technique that has come into use in political science because of the influence of economic theorists is the technique of spatial models. A *spatial model* pictorially represents the people of a given society along a single policy dimension, placing each individual at the position he is assumed to prefer. The classical application of such a model in connection with political problems is found in Anthony Downs's *Economic Theory of Democracy*.[46]

Based on the assumption that on a liberal–conservative dimension the majority of voters fall toward the center, Downs suggested that political parties would also tend toward moderate positions to maximize their votes.[47] However, if the distribution is bimodal, with large extremes and few voters in the middle, the parties will remain widely separated. This behavior is due to the threat of abstention by extremist voters, or even the threat of a third-party movement, if the existing parties get too close together ideologically. Downs also suggests that the expansion of the franchise is likely to change the picture dramatically, perhaps providing an auspicious time for the development of a new party.[48]

A more recent application of spatial models in political science is the work of *Robert Axelrod*, who defines the conflict of interest in a society as equal to the variance of the distribution of the population along a policy dimension.[49] He then applies this method of analysis to (1) the apportionment of representatives in a society, and (2) the theory of cross-cutting and overlapping cleavages. With respect to apportionment, Axelrod demonstrates that a representative system with internally homogeneous districts will concentrate conflict of interest in the legislature, whereas a system that draws districts *across* ethnic, geographical, or cultural lines will be more homogeneous at the legislative level.

Assuming that a person's preferred policy position is the average of the positions of the social groups of which he is a member, Axelrod shows that cross-cutting cleavages will be expected to produce a unimodal distribution approximating normality, while overlapping cleavages will produce a bimodal distribution with a larger standard deviation. This implies that conflict of interest is higher in a society with overlapping cleavages than in one with cross-cultural cleavages.

Perhaps a major drawback of spatial models is their focus on a single issue or policy dimension. At times such a focus may obscure the complexity of reality. In the early stages of theory development, however, spatial models can be quite valuable in illustrating dramatically some basic insights into the political process.

CRITIQUE

Economic concepts can be useful in formulating concepts of political problems. The idea of rational political man making decisions in the political realm and employing the kinds of utility maximization assumption postulated for similar models of economic man has considerable attractiveness. Michael Shapiro illustrates some of these prospects with his data showing the rationality of support for presidential candidates Humphrey, McCarthy, Kennedy, Nixon, and Rockefeller in 1968, based on party, personal qualities, issues, and interpersonal cues.[50] Some reservations, however, must be stated. First, it is often difficult to find in politics directly analogous situations to allow the fruitful application of economic concepts and hypotheses. Any such hypothesis, even if already tested empirically with respect to economic questions, must be submitted to a further test using operationalized political variables. In terms of rationality, for example, we can easily be led to erroneous conclusions if we assume too much about similarities in the scope and depth of the information available to individual decision makers. Significant differences in the average level of uncertainty about potential outcomes can have a great impact on how closely decisions and decision making can be made to fit a rational model. This factor may have significant influence on the value of any predictions based on this assumption. Furthermore, key political decision makers often cannot wait for a good rate of exchange. Emergency situations, such as the Cuban missile crisis or the *Pueblo* incident offer little time for changes in what must be described as a unfavorable price situation. Inaction or delay in such cases is in itself an irreversible decision.

A second crucial problem lies in the area of operationalization and measurement. It is much easier to measure rates of income or unemployment than it is to measure political costs and resources. Similarly, political units of exchange are generally much more difficult to quantify than are economic units of exchange. Voting is one political variable that can be quantified quite easily, and perhaps this is why voting studies are stressed in research into political rationality. Lack of an effective market mechanism and recognized political currencies thus greatly hinders efforts to apply economic-type models in political science.

Third, many economic concepts and approaches are extremely limited in scope. Game theory, for example, is very difficult to apply to the analysis of complex, multidimensional issues. The concepts of costs and resources, developed specifically in connection with economic problems, are best used by political scientists in specific situations in which the concepts can be easily identified and will remain stable over time. Finally, the contents of concepts such as costs and resources are especially subject to cultural relativity. An hour of time may be an insignificant thing for a tropical islander to give up, but a Western or Japanese businessman would place high value on the same unit. Clean water may be an extremely valuable resource in one society, but in another it may be of negligible economic cost.

The above-mentioned concerns are important and must be kept in mind. Nevertheless, the potential value of applying concepts and techniques developed in economics to the study of political problems has not nearly been realized.

NOTES

[1] Paul A. Samuelson, *Economics: An Introductory Analysis*, 5th ed., (New York: McGraw-Hill, 1961), p. 6.

[2] Rationality has been appearing with increasing frequency in the titles of articles published by the *American Political Science Review*. Such articles appeared in four out of five issues in 1969 and early 1970.

[3] Such concerns involve reference to the level of information available to the decision maker: whether he has access to complete information about alternatives, outcomes, and the preferences of other relevant actors; or whether he is able to document only a very limited range of known alternative actions. Michael Shapiro, "Rational Political Man: A Synthesis of Economic and Social-Psychological Perspectives," *American Political Science Review*, vol. 63, no. 4 (December 1969), pp. 1106–1119.

[4] Anthony Downs, *An Economic Theory of Democracy*, (New York: Harper & Row, 1957).

[5] Ibid. pp. 260–276.

[6] Mancur Olson, Jr., *The Logic of Collective Action: Public Goods and the Theory of Groups* (Cambridge, Mass.: Harvard University Press, Schocken paperback edition, p. 86.

[7] Ibid., p. 86.

[8] Robert A. Dahl and Charles Linblom, *Politics, Economics, and Welfare* (New York: Harper Torchbook, Harper & Row, 1953), pp. 89–90.

[9] See R. D. Luce and H. Raiffa, *Games and Decisions* (New York: Wiley, 1957).

[10] In Kenneth Arrow, *Social Choice and Individual Values* (New York: Wiley, 1951), p. 60.

[11] James S. Coleman, "The Possibility of a Social Welfare Function," *American Economic Review*, vol. 56, no. 5 (December 1966), pp. 1105–1122.

[12] Arrow, *Social Choice and Individual Values*, p. 91.

[13] See, for example, S. T. Possony, "Foreign Policy and Rationality," *Orbis*, vol. 12. no. 1 (Spring 1968), pp. 132–160.

[14] William H. Riker and William Zavoina, "Rational Behavior in Politics: Evidence from a Three-Person Game," *American Political Science Review*, vol. 64, no. 1 (March 1970), pp. 48–60.

[15] Arthur Goldberg, "Social Determinism and Rationality as Bases of Party Identification," *American Political Science Review*, vol. 63, no. 1 (March 1969), pp. 5–25.

[16] See, for example, Allen M. Shinn, Jr., "An Application of Psycho-Physical Scaling Techniques to the Measurement of National Power," *Journal of Politics*, vol. 31, no. 4 (November 1969), pp. 932–951.

[17] Robert A. Dahl, *Who Governs?* (New Haven, Conn.: Yale University Press, 1961), pp. 223–245.

[18] See, for example, Sanford A. Mosh, "The Pathology of Democracy in Latin America: An Economist's Point of View," *American Political Science Review*, vol. 44, no. 1 (March 1950), pp. 129–142.

[19] Michael Lipsky, "Protest as a Political Resource," *American Political Science Review*, vol. 62, no. 4 (December 1968), pp. 1144–1158.

[20] See, for example, Karl W. Deutsch, "Toward an Inventory of Basic Trends and Patterns in Comparative and International Politics," *American Political Science Review*, vol. 54 (1960), pp. 34–57; Gabrial A. Almond and G. B. Powell, Jr., *Comparative Politics: A Developmental Approach* (Boston and Toronto: Little, Brown, 1966), especially pp. 190–212.

[21] Dahl, *Who Governs?* pp. 235–240.

[22] J. M. Mitchell and W. C. Mitchell, *Political Analysis and Public Policy* (Skokie, Ill.: Rand McNally, 1969). See R. M. Goldman, "A Transactional Theory of Political Integration and Arms Control," *American Political Science Review*, vol. 63, no. 3 (September 1969), pp. 719–733, for a discussion of this context.

[23] See R. L. Curry, Jr., and L. L. Wade, *A Theory of Political Exchange* (Englewood Cliffs, N.J.: Prentice-Hall, 1968).

[24] See Goldman, "A Transactional Theory. . . ," pp. 726–729.

[25] Dahl and Lindblom, *Politics, Economics, and Welfare*, pp. 89–92.

[26] See J. M. and W. C. Mitchell, *Political Analysis and Public Policy*, chap. 5, "The Distribution of Costs," pp. 167–206.

[27] See Dahl and Lindblom, *Politics Economics, and Welfare*, pp. 247–271.

[28] See James M. Buchanan and Gordon Tullock, *The Calculus of Consent* (Ann Arbor: University of Michigan Press, 1962) for a further discussion of costs in connection with decisions of bargaining.

[29] J. S. Coleman, "Foundations for a Theory of Collective Decisions," *American Journal of Sociology*, vol. 71, no. 6 (May 1, 1966), pp. 615–627.

[30] Dahl and Lindblom, *Politics, Economics, and Welfare*, p. 472.

[31] Thomas C. Schelling, *The Strategy of Conflict*, (New York: Oxford University Press, 1963), p. 22.

[32] Ibid., p. 60.

[33] Curry and Wade, *A Theory of Political Exchange* pp. 39–48.

[34] See Alfred Kuhn, *The Study of Society*, chaps. 17–20 for a discussion of this area. Also Alfred Kuhn, *The Structure of Scientific Revolutions* (Chicago: University of Chicago Press, 1962).

[35] See Thomas C. Schelling, *The Strategy of Conflict*, pp. 35–46, for a fuller discussion of the importance of threats and promises.

[36] See, for example, Martin Shubik, "Game Theory and the Study of Social Behavior: An Introductory Exposition," in *Game Theory and Related Approaches to Social Behavior*, Martin Shubik, ed. (New York: Wiley, 1964), pp. 3–77.

[37] A matrix is any rectangular array of numbers or sequence of numbers.

$$\begin{bmatrix} 1 & 2 \\ 3 & 4 \end{bmatrix}$$ is a matrix, as are 5.1 to 5.5 on pages 127–129. 5.1 is a

pay-off matrix, since it specifies assumed pay-offs for different actors as a result of differing combinations of actions.

[38] It can be established that any constant-sum game is equivalent for the purposes of analysis to the zero-sum game formed by subtracting from each value or pay-off an amount equal to the total of the pay-offs to all players or actors in the game situation for any one call of the matrix, divided by the number of players.

[39] Kenneth Boulding, *Conflict and Defense: A General Theory*, (New York: Harper & Row, 1963), pp. 49–53.

[40] This is a famous problem in game theory. Game theoretic formulation of this problem shows it to be of the same form as the above example, where each finds it rational to take a negative option if he does not know what the other is going to do, although it would be better for both if they could reach an agreement.

[41] Buchanan and Tullock, *The Calculus of Consent*, 1967 printing, especially pp. 147–169.

[42] Ibid. This discussion is found in chaps. 11–13, pp. 170–210.

[43] See Anatol Rapaport, *N-Person Game Theory* (Ann Arbor: University of Michigan Press, 1970).

[44] Riker, *The Theory of Political Coalitions*.

[45] Shubik also discusses a variety of other games, including formulations in which one or both of the participants is indifferent to the outcome. See also Thomas C. Schelling, *The Strategy of Conflict*, 150–

158. Schelling also discusses the use of randomized commitments, which in a conflict situation prevent an opponent with a clear advantage from fully exploiting that advantage.

46 Anthony Downs, *An Economic Theory of Democracy*, see particularly chap. 8, pp. 114–141.

47 Ibid., p. 118.

48 Ibid., p. 129; see also Donald E. Stokes, "Spatial Models of Party Competition," *American Political Science Review*, vol. 57 (1963), pp. 368–377, for a critique and extension of Downs's work.

49 Robert Axelrod, *Conflict of Interest: A Theory of Divergent Goals with Applications to Politics* (Chicago: Markham, 1970), pp. 44–64.

50 Michael Shapiro, "Rational Political Man."

Psychology and Politics

Since predicting politics often involves predicting human behavior, psychology might seem to be a natural source of insights for political investigations. Nevertheless, political scientists have been reluctant and fretful in their application of psychological concepts to political analysis. Rather than come to grips with psychological politics, they have tried to avoid psychological variables by stressing the impact of environmental pressures on the shaping of human behavior. Indeed, systems analysis, structural functionalism, power, communication, "rationality," and other concepts surveyed in the preceding chapters represent explicit attempts by social scientists to predict political behavior without becoming enmeshed in the intricacies of the human psyche.

Several of the most vital "political questions," however, are inherently psychological. How do individuals learn their basic political attitudes? How do they form opinions? How can opinions be changed? How do individuals make decisions? Why do populations that have traditionally been docile suddenly overwhelm the dominant system with demands for change? Why are radicals radical, and authoritarians authoritarian?

As a general proposition, both the range and accuracy of political analysis are likely to benefit as political scientists develop the ability to grapple with the psychological as well as the environmental determinants of political behavior.

This is not to suggest that psychological variables are the overriding determinants of political behavior, but rather, as J. Milton Yinger hypothesizes, that complex human acts such as political, social, and economic behavior are determined by the *field* in which the individual's cultural, environmental, personality, and biological forces interact.[1] (See Figure 6.1.)

According to Figure 6.1, for example, nonvoting among Negroes in the rural South might well be explained by any

Illustrative Research Areas[1]

	Perception	Illness	Suicide	Talent	Discrimination	Economic Behavior	Political Behavior	Religious Behavior	Motivation	Socialization
Biology										
Psychology										
Sociology										
Culturology										

Figure 6.1 Illustrative research areas.
(J. Milton Yinger, *Toward a Field Theory of Behavior.*
New York: McGraw-Hill, 1965, p. 28.)

of the four categories in the left-hand column: Biology, Psychology, Sociology, or Culturology. Biologically, substandard diets and high incidence of disease are well-established causes of political lethargy. Psychologically, large segments of the Negro population have "given up hope" of gaining equality with the white community through elections and feel *alienated* from the political system under which they live. Sociologically, the class system erects serious obstacles to black voting, thus thwarting numerous laws designed to ensure fair voting practices. Culturally, the *norms* and *mores* in many rural black communities urge their members to "get along with" and "don't mess with" whitey.

This chapter surveys a variety of psychological concepts of particular relevance to the study of political behavior and illustrates their application by political scientists. The discussion of psychology and politics should be viewed as stressing one of several essential dimensions to political analysis rather than as a "new" or distinct approach to political science. Suggesting that all political phenomena could be reduced to psychological explanations (psychologizing) would be as grave an error as ignoring psychological factors altogether.

SOME NECESSARY BACKGROUND

Before beginning to examine the political relevance of various psychological concepts, let us survey the background of certain popular yet rather ambiguous concepts that are used by political scientists.

To many psychologists, as well as to a growing number of political scientists the psyche is a complex "black box" filled with such entities as *self-needs, drives, ego,* and *super-ego,* few of them directly observable, but all seeming to have an important impact on human behavior.

Every individual, from earliest childhood, develops a *self-concept*—an *identity*—a mental image of who and what he is and of precisely how he fits into the world around him.[2] Am I bright, am I desirable, am I pretty, am I powerful, am I a good son, am I a good father, a good worker?

The individual develops his self-concept by observing the reactions of other people. Other people, to cite Cooley's famous analogy, serve as a "looking glass" from which the individual gathers images of what he is and how he's doing.[3] "I am beautiful because people say I am beautiful"; "I am intelligent because I score high on examinations and receive good grades"; "I am strong because people defer to my wishes and fear to oppose me." As later sections illustrate, an individual's self-concept can have a profound effect on his political behavior.

Individuals also possess *needs* and *drives*. Physical needs such as food and sex have long been recognized. For students of personality, however, the individual is additionally burdened with a variety of social and psychological needs. For example, people seem to have an abiding need for security, stability, and order.[4] They prefer a universe that is tight and orderly; a personal world in which everything fits, in which all the rules are known and in which there are few surprises.

Individuals also need to belong: to be wanted, loved, accepted, respected, and appreciated. Experiments with monkeys and other higher primates demonstrate that offspring removed from their parents and reared without affection do not match the physical development of their socially reared brethren.[5]

Just as individuals *need* to be well regarded by others, they also *need* to think well of themselves. Several studies suggest that people can think poorly of themselves only at the expense of their own well-being.[6] Furthermore, individuals who do not think well of themselves find it difficult to relate effectively to others.[7]

So pressing is the need for self-acceptance that many psychologists believe that the individual develops not only a *self-concept*, but also an *idealized self-concept*: a coherent, if frequently unrealistic, vision of his virtues, capabilities, and values.[8] When the image in the mirror diverges too sharply from the idealized self-concept, many people will risk losing touch with reality rather than accept their own inadequacy.

Psychologists have also observed that considerable human energy is expended in pursuit of developmental goals (i.e., toward developing the mind and body to the greatest extent possible). On this basis it has been suggested that individuals possess self-actualization needs in addition to the biologic and psychologic needs just described.[9] Although a general striving for achievement has been noted, delineations of actualization needs have been somewhat nebulous.[10]

When one or more of an individual's needs are being imperfectly met, a state of disequilibrium exists, and "psychic energy" or *drive* is released to meet the deprived need and to restore the body to a state of equilibrium or "homeostasis." Thus when you become "hungry," the drive to eat becomes the overwhelming focus of your activity until the *need state* has been reduced.[11] Similarly, individuals whose needs for stability, security, acceptance, or achievement are inadequately satisfied become "unbalanced" in their pursuit of a stable, secure environment, in their search for acceptance and belonging, and in their efforts to achieve.

The link between need states and political behavior is often direct and readily observed. It is not unusual for individuals lacking in self-assurance and self-confidence to be swayed by the appeals of authoritarian movements promising a world of order and stability, in which one has only to obey the rules to survive. Individuals who feel rejected often turn to the fanatical solidarity of extremist movements to acquire the sense of belonging and acceptance that society has denied them. Frequently, too, individuals with accentuated needs for recognition or achievement find that political activity provides the recognition they crave. Before elaborating the political application of *needs* and *drives*, however, we must introduce the very nebulous concepts of ego and super-ego.

The *ego* is a "psychic mechanism" that evolves to supervise and direct the gratification of human needs in a realistic manner.[12] The ego occupies a position akin to that of a ship's pilot. It gives conscious expression to the individual's wants, and it is also responsible for gratifying those wants and desires in a manner consonant both with reality and with the norms of society. The ego is charged with maximizing the individual's gratifications while simultaneously protecting him from self-destruction through the unbridled pursuit of his needs.

The *super-ego*, for all practical purposes, is the individual's conscience.[13] When "ego" would say "The penalties for theft and the probabilities of getting caught are excessive and not worth the risk," the superego would add that theft is morally wrong.

The position of the ego, however, is often precarious. What if *drives* for need gratification become overwhelming? What if the social and moral restraints of one's society are so rigid that the normal expression of sexual and other drives is precluded? What if reality is so harsh that nondestructive paths to gratification cannot be found? In short, what if the pilot "ego" cannot steer a clear course between the conflicting demands of needs, super-ego, and reality? The answer is that *ego* resorts to a variety of *defense mechanisms*, most of them involving either the distortion of reality or the substitution of one form of gratification for another. The *defense mechanisms* outlined below are of particular relevance to political behavior.

Rationalization is essentially the attempt to relieve the pangs of conscience or super-ego by justifying undesirable acts in terms acceptable to the super-ego. "I'm not really opposed to integration, but I have to get along with my neighbors."

Projection is the attempt to placate the pangs of conscience by attributing one's own undesirable motives to others. "He was so hostile, I had no alternative but to hit him."

Displacement is the unconscious transfer of emotions from

one object to another. The man who cannot kick his boss, kicks his dog instead. Intensely prejudiced people are often displacing the hostility generated by their own failures onto minorities such as Negroes or Jews. Displacement seldom eliminates the source of the individual's anxiety, but it provides temporary relief and spares ego the necessity of acknowledging personal shortcomings.

It should be noted in passing that most people indulge in defensive behavior at one time or another. The political relevance of these other forms of defensive behavior is illustrated shortly.

POLITICS AND NEED-BASED PSYCHOLOGY

The political applications of *need-* and *ego*-based concepts have been many and varied. In *Political Thinking and Political Consciousness*, Robert E. Lane employs depth interviews of 24 male college students to explain a wide variety of political behavior in terms of needs and drives. The "need to be liked" is seen by Lane as follows:[14]

Need	A. *Obstacles to Easy Friendship* *Mediating Element*	*Political Expression*
Need to be liked	Intellectuality, especially at an early age, where cognitive responses stifle casual, playful, affective responses; both cause and effect of social anxiety.	Painful indecision in politics; ambivalence; hedging, but rarely withdrawal.
Need to be liked	Fear of intimacy combining with need for reassurance about likeability; tendency to maintain distance between self and others and to symbolize people.	Bid for the affection of distinct underdogs; religious racial tolerance and symbolic equalitarianism.
Need to be liked	Blockages and strain in interpersonal relations with self-confident elites (possibly reflecting one kind of authority tension).	Selection of lower status, less "important" clienteles, audience, welfare policy targets.
	B. *Validating the Self-* *Mediating Element*	
Need to be liked	Self-doubt and intense need for self-validation combined with self-conscious interpersonal skills.	Popularity: Vote solicitation on "clean-cut" reference lines. Votes as affirmation of acceptability.

Need to be liked	A sense of lost momentum in the drive for "success," especially status among peers, memories of former glories, fears of loss of drive and motivation.	Political choice less "autonomous" and more in the service of ambition and opportunity.
Need to be liked	Ambivalent social identity creating and reflecting social anxiety; identification denied, flaunted, used in "the social encounter."	Political thought reflecting (1) elements of a dialogue with an internal opposition; (2) a flexible, but often intense commitment.
Need to be liked	Rejection (and quasi-repression) of unacceptable thoughts, hence search for resolution formula.	Pseudoconformity to license the guilty idea; screen confession of "weakness" in face of pressure.

Lane has suggested in various works that the concepts of ego- and need-based psychology are relevant to all forms of political behavior. The utilization of need and ego concepts by most social and political scientists, however, has stressed the relationship between need deprivation and extremist politics. This trend began some 20 years ago with the publication of *The Authoritarian Personality*, an exhaustive study of fascist tendencies.[15] The authors believe that the roots of authoritarianism are psychological and that individuals who tend toward right-wing extremism also manifest strong feelings of isolation, self-doubt, and inadequacy, and an exaggerated need for security, stability, and reassurance. To gain security and reassurance, authoritarian personalities are said to indulge in the following behaviors:

a. *Conventionalism.* Rigid adherence to conventional, middle-class values.
b. *Authoritarian submission.* Submissive, uncritical attitude toward idealized moral authorities of the ingroup.
c. *Authoritarian aggression.* Tendency to be on the look-out for, and to condemn, reject, and punish people who violate conventional values.
d. *Anti-intraception.* Opposition to the subjective, the imaginative, the tender-minded.

e. *Superstition and stereotype.* The belief in mystical determinants of the individual's fate; the disposition to think in rigid categories.

f. *Power and "toughness."* Preoccupation with the dominance–submission, strong–weak, leader–follower dimension identification with power figures; overemphasis upon the conventionalized attributes of the ego; exaggerated assertion of strength and toughness.

g. *Destructiveness and cynicism.* Generalized hostility, vilification of the human.

h. *Projectivity.* The disposition to believe that wild and dangerous things go on in the world; the projection outwards of unconscious emotional impulses.

i. *Sex.* Exaggerated concern with sexual "goings-on."[16]

The Authoritarian Personality was severely criticized on various methodological grounds; it was also attacked as being hypersensitive to right-wing extremism and insufficiently sensitive to extremism of the left.[17] The work nevertheless stands as a classic application of psychological variables to political phenomena.

Among the many studies spawned by *The Authoritarian Personality* were McCloskey's efforts to establish personality correlates of liberalism and conservatism. His results were markedly similar to those of Adorno and his colleagues.

Intelligence. One of the clearest findings in both studies [Adorno and Herbert McCloskey] is that contrary to claim, conservatism is not the preferred doctrine of the intellectual elite or of the more intelligent segments of the population, but the reverse. By every measure available to us, conservative beliefs are found most frequently among the uninformed, the poorly educated, and so far as we can determine, the less intelligent.

Conservatism, in our society at least, appears to be far more characteristic of social isolates, of people who think poorly of themselves, who suffer personal disgruntlement and frustration, who are submissive, timid, and wanting in confidence, who lack a clear sense of direction and purpose, who are uncertain about their values, and who are generally bewildered by the alarming task of having to thread their way through a society which seems to them too complex to fathom.

Of the four liberal–conservative classifications, the extreme conservatives are easily the most hostile and suspicious, the most rigid and compulsive, the quickest to condemn others for their imperfections or weaknesses, the most intolerant, the most easily moved to scorn and disappointment in others, the most inflexible and unyielding in their perceptions and judgments. Although aggressively critical of the shortcomings of others, they are unusually defensive and armored in the protection of their own ego needs. Poorly integrated psychologically, anxious, often perceiving themselves as inadequate, and subject to excessive feelings of guilt, they seem inclined to project onto others the traits they most dislike or fear in themselves.[18]

Needs for belonging, security, and self-regard have also been cited as major causes for "working-class authoritarianism," and for membership in extremist parties of the left. In analyzing the behavior of former members of Communist parties on four continents, Almond found that one of the primary appeals of the Communist party was its image of strength, comradeship, unity, and imortality:

It would also appear that Communism may appeal to persons who feel rejected or are rejected by their environments. The image of the Communist militant is of a dignified, special person, dedicated, strong, confident of the future, a man who knows his objectives, does his duty without hesitation. These aspects of Communism have an obvious attraction for persons who carry within themselves feelings of being weak and unworthy as a consequence of early childhood experiences, as well as for persons who have been objectively rejected by their environments. The Negro, the Jew, the foreign-born, and the first-generation native-born, the unemployed, the native intellectual in a colonial country, may respond to their social situation by feeling rejected, unworthy, lacking in dignity and esteem. In this sense, any negatively discriminated status may contribute to susceptibility. Throughout the interviews, even when neurotic problems were not indicated, this theme of rejection occurred with some frequency. In other cases, the emphasis was on weakness and inadequacy; in others, on ugliness, unworthiness, unassimilability.[19]

There can be little doubt that extremist politics offers marginal individuals a means of achieving security, acceptance, and ego support. It would be a serious mistake, however, to view *need disequilibrium* as a disorder limited to the "lunatic fringe." Personality psychologists would argue that most individuals harbor latent fears of rejection, inferiority, and insecurity—fears that are repressed as socially undesirable as long as the individual is well integrated into his society and receives feelings of security, acceptance, and self-worth from his friends, family, and job.[20]

But what happens to suppressed feelings of insecurity, inadequacy, and rejection when the world suddenly comes apart at the seams, when the well-integrated individual finds his world of normality replaced by a world of crisis and disorganization? Suddenly everyone, by force of circumstances, becomes marginal. As need deprivation increases, suppressed drives overwhelm the super-ego and become manifest. It is thus that both Gerth and Lasswell explain the rise of Nazism in Germany.

Those placed on the disadvantaged side of life always tend to be interested in some sort of salvation which breaks through the routines associated with their deprivation. Such "unsuccessful" persons were to be found in every stratum of German society. Princes without thrones, indebted and subsidized landlords, indebted farmers, virtually bankrupt industrialists, impoverished shopkeepers and artisans, doctors without patients, lawyers without clients, writers without readers, unemployed teachers, and unemployed manual and white-collar workers joined the movement. National Socialism as a salvationary movement exercised an especially strong attraction on the "old" and "new" middle classes, especially in those strata where substantive rationality is least developed, and will be the most highly represented among those seeking salvation by quasi-miraculous means—or at least by methods which break through the routines which account for their deprivation.[21]

Hitler has come to stand for the reaffirmation of the cardinal moral virtues whose neglect has weakened the whole fiber of the German nation. Putrid literature, putrid drama, putrid practices are imputed to the foul Jew who desecrated the homeland whose hospitality he so long enjoyed. The stress of battle, undernourishment, inflation, and unemployment during these recent eventful years has exposed many men and women to "temptations" which they could not resist, and the accumulated weight of guilt arising from these irregularities drives many of them into acts of expiation. In some measure the "awakening of Germany" is a cleansing gesture of aspiration for a feeling of moral worth, and the Jew is the sacrificial ram.

Such is the meaning of the emphasis in Hitler's public personality upon abstinence from wine, women and excess; this is the clue to the appeal of the humourless gravity which is one of his most obvious traits.[22]

By identifying with Hitler, members of the increasingly marginal German middle class not only gained security and a renewed sense of purpose, they also found a means of purging themselves of feelings of guilt and failure by *displacing* and *projecting* their guilt onto the Jewish minority, a process frequently referred to as *scapegoating*.[23]

IDENTITY AND IDENTIFICATION

The political applications of need- and ego-based psychology can be further extended by adding the concepts of identity and identification.

As children go about the task of building a "self" or an "identity," they may be thought of as experiencing an *identity crisis*.[24] They are not entirely sure who or what they are or precisely how they fit into their universe. To complicate matters, the rules always seem to be changing. No sooner do they adjust to their parents than they are thrown into a classroom and forced to redefine their identity in terms of peers and teachers. With the arrival of adolescence they must somehow cope with members of the opposite sex. As they progress through high school and college and into the business world, they find that behavior tolerated at age 15 is scorned and ridiculed at age 18—that teenagers must become adults.

The needs for security, acceptance, and self-respect all drive the individual to work out a stable self-concept or identity. In response to this drive for identity, the individual is in constant search for *role cues*: "What am I expected to do, and how do I do it."[25]

The obvious approach to this problem is to imitate the behavior of those who seem to know, particularly those in positions of authority. Thus at the earliest levels, children work out an identity by copying their parents, including parental attitudes, values, and behavior. Children not only copy their parents' behavior and attitudes, but they also make them part of their own identity; that is, they *internalize* their parents' values and behavior.

The process of copying and internalizing the behavior, attitudes, and values of another individual or object is referred to as *identification*. When a child identifies with a parent, or when an individual *identifies* with a political or military "strong man," he sees himself as possessing all the virtues of the identification object, and he shares in that object's glories as if they were his own. The process of identification gives the weak individual, the uncertain individual, and the insecure individual an identity—a purpose, a source of pride, and a stable point of reference. In terms of the concepts discussed earlier, the attitudes and behavior of identification objects becomes part of the individual's ideal self. The individual begins to see himself as the object (ideal-self) and to establish the identification object's behavior as his own moral code.

One of the major political applications of the concept of *identification* is the study of political *socialization*—the process by which individuals acquire their basic political attitudes and loyalties. (Operant conditioning as an approach to socialization is discussed on pp. 164–167.)

Children learn how to become adults largely through identifying with their parents. An integral part of this learning process is the acquisition of parental attitudes on politics. If the parents display strong feelings of trust and loyalty toward the political system, the children will be predisposed to do likewise. The same, of course, is true of parental attitudes of distrust and alienation.

Closely related to the process of identification is the tendency of children to *transfer* attitudes developed toward their parents to other figures of authority. In a study of 12,000 American children between the ages of 7 and 14, Easton and Dennis found evaluations of "father power" to be the best predictor of the child's evaluation of "presidential power." Children who rated their father "low" on power also tended to rate the President "low" on power.[26]

In many of the developing nations in which mass education and broad exposure to the mass media have yet to be established, the family remains the primary agent of political socialization. In more developed states, the basic attitudes instilled through identification with the parents are modified by a host of additional socializing agents including schools, peers, political parties, the mass media, and various forms of government propaganda. Attitudes toward the political system also develop in response to the individual's ever-increasing accumulation of experience and information concerning the political system and its impact on his life.

Indeed, just how important the role of the family may be in the political socialization of the child is currently a subject of some debate. In their study of 17,000 elementary children, grades two through eight, Hess and Torney found the impact of the school to be perhaps more important than that of the family in shaping the child's political attitudes. They summarize their research as follows:

From the viewpoint of the totality of socialization into the political system, these results indicate that the effectiveness of the family in transmitting attitudes has been overestimated in previous research. The family transmits preference for a political party, but in most other areas its most effective role is to support other institutions in teaching political information and orientations. Clearcut similarities among children in the same family are confined to partisanship and related attitudes, such as feelings of distress or pleasure over the outcome of an election campaign. Aside from party preference, the influence of the family seems to be primarily indirect and to influence attitudes toward authority, rules, and compliance.

There is some relationship between family structure and the child's interest in the political system. Children who see their fathers as powerful tend to be more informed and interested in political matters; children who see their mothers as the dominant authority in the family tend to be less interested in politics and to acquire attitudes at a later period than do children who see the father as the dominant parent or see both parents as equal in authority.

The school apparently plays the largest part in teaching attitudes, conceptions, and beliefs about the operation of the political system. While it may be argued that the family contributes much to the socialization that goes into basic loyalty to the country, the school gives content, information, and concepts which expand and elaborate these early feelings of attachment.[27]

The concept of identification has also been useful in analyzing the behavior of the political fanatic—the "true believer."

Many of the marginal individuals discussed earlier are "true believers"—individuals lacking in security, acceptance, and self-regard; individuals suffering from an identity crisis. Identifying with extremist movements of the left or right or becoming a devotee of a charismatic leader or demagogue provides the marginal individual with a psychic crutch. His life is suddenly filled with a sense of meaning and purpose. He has gained acceptance. Having found truth in the ideology of the party or the person of the leader, he acquires self-esteem and self-assurance in this new role as "disciple." As discussed in *The Appeals of Communism*:

While hostility and resentment appear to be all-pervasive themes in the appeal of Communism, the attractions of the party typically involve other emotional problems and needs. . . . In the classics and in the Communist media of communication there is constant emphasis on organization, community, relatedness. The ideal image of the Communist conveys the impression of a man who has his place in the meaningful progression of time, and who is surrounded by steadfast and loyal comrades. The Communist militant is not only related to a group; he also shares in a kind of mystical body, he merges himself in the *corpus mysticum* of the party, acquires a large identity from it and even a sense of immortality. This stress upon union and unity, sharing in communion and community, has a special impact upon those who are unrelated or inadequately related to their fellowmen, upon the lonely and the isolated. It can appeal to the one whose loneliness is situational—for example, to the college freshman away from home for the first time, who may lack the necessary introductions and contacts—as well as to the one whose loneliness is self-imposed, who rejects and withdraws from others because of some deep distrust of men, some fear of being improperly used and hurt.[28]

In stable societies "identity seekers" represent a minor though potentially dangerous segment of the population. However, political scientists working in the developing regions suggest that identity crises are a widespread phenomenon in areas experiencing the trauma of intense social and technological change. The following passage from Colin

M. Turnbull's *The Lonely African* provides a vivid description of this process in the African context.

> In the cities the African has been consistently taught to be ashamed of his tribal past and his religious beliefs, taught that he was a savage and a sinner, and often he has not learned otherwise. Nor has his attempt to become a black-skinned white man met with much success. In rural areas those who are not converted, either to Christianity or to a belief that the new world of the white man is the ideal to strive after, are little better off. Their faith in the old is shaken by the demonstrably superior power of the new, and insofar as it is made impossible for them to perform all the secular and ritual activities that are considered pleasing to the ancestors, they feel that their life in the afterworld is likely to be equally unsuccessful and unpleasing.
>
> Individuals find their own solutions to the dilemma, but the basic solidarity has been broken. Administrators tend to say that detribalization is a good thing, but they are thinking only in terms of administrative convenience. Detribalization brings with it the complete breakdown of moral and spiritual values, and separates each individual from his fellows.[29]

Identity crises aside, it is a rare individual who does not, to some extent, identify with groups, such as athletic teams, tribes, civic clubs, political parties, religions, ideologies, and nations. The ecstasy or depression that acccompanies the fortunes of most football teams provides a very common example of identification by individuals with a group or institutional object. Why, for instance, should so much energy be spent on being "number one" unless individuals who identify with the team can vicariously fantasize that they, too, are "number one"?

Doob suggests that nationalism is the same order of phenomenon.[30] When individuals identify with a nation-state, they in fact develop an ego involvement with the state (or other group) and its successes. *We* Americans are powerful, honest, industrious, creative, and generally superior; therefore, *I* am a powerful, honest, industrious, creative, and generally superior individual. The reasoning may be faulty, but the thrill is tremendous. The more intensely individuals identify with a nation, the greater the ability of national leaders to use symbols (e.g., flags, the Constitution, the Bill of Rights, Uncle Sam) to mobilize them in pursuit of goals the elite deem desirable.

Nationalism, however, is an elusive concept. Individuals identify with a variety of groups simultaneously. In most countries a typical citizen might identify with his family, his club, his school, his home town, his province, his geographic region, his religion, his ethnic group, his economic class, and his political party, as well as his country. Which comes first? Does the state come before the church, or the church before the state? Are identifications with the political party, the ethnic group, or the region more intense than identification with the nation?

When identifications with the nation are more intense than parochial identifications—when a majority of the population puts the state before all other groups—the state is psychologically or culturally *integrated.*

Few states in the world are so well integrated that parochial loyalties do not conflict with national loyalties on certain issues. During the 1970s, for example, nationalistic appeals by political leaders for support of the country's objectives in Vietnam were not sufficient to convince a large portion of the American public that the government's claims were justified. Much popular resistance was due to conflicting parochial values. Many clergymen in the United States contended that the values of a citizen's faith take precedence over the military goals of national leadership. Similarly, many black leaders opposed the war on the grounds that the needs of the black community deserved priority over the unrelated goals of the national leadership. In both instances, the symbols being purveyed by parochial leaders were more salient to much of the population than the national symbols purveyed by national leaders. The influence of parochial leaders might have been greater yet if the symbols associated with the black and antiwar movements had not been beset with the vagueness, ambiguity, and conflict so characteristic of the movements themselves.

Also falling under the general rubric of identification is the concept of *empathy. Empathy*, as defined by Daniel Lerner, is the ability to be highly mobile—to move freely from one situation to another, and to be able to "put oneself in another's shoes." The author elaborates:

We are interested in empathy as the inner mechanism which enables newly mobile persons to *operate efficiently* in a changing world. Empathy, to simplify the matter, is the capacity to see oneself in the other fellow's situation. This is an indispensable skill for people moving out of traditional settings. Ability to empathize may make all the difference, for example, when the newly mobile persons are villagers who grew up knowing all the extant individuals, roles and relationships in their environment. Outside his village or tribe, each must meet new individuals, recognize new roles, and learn new relationships involving himself. . . . Our interest is to clarify the process whereby the high empathizer tends to become also the cash customer, the radio listener, the voter.[31]

Empathy, according to Lerner, is acquired by exposure to a broad range of information and personal experiences. High levels of literacy, urbanization, and exposure to mass media are all related to high levels of empathy. As empathy increases, the ability of the individual to have political opinions and to effectively participate in political life also increases. The text of Lerner's interviews provides a vivid picture of "low empathy" individuals:

. . . This came out when Tosun asked another of his projective questions: "If you could not live in Turkey, where would you want to live?" The standard reply of the villagers was that they would not live, could not imagine living, anywhere else. The forced choice simply was ignored.

When Tosun persisted ("Suppose you *had* to leave Turkey?") he teased an extreme reaction out of some Balgati. The shepherd, like several other wholly routinized personalities, finally replied that he would rather kill himself. The constricted peasant can more easily imagine destroying the self than relocating it in an unknown, i.e., frightful, setting.[32]

Taken together, the works of Doob and Lerner lead us to state the following pair of propositions: (1) nationalism is based on the identification of the individual with the institutions and symbols of the nation, and (2) before an individual can identify with the institutions and symbols of the nation he must, through education (media) or experience, understand what it means to be part of a nation and how national institutions directly influence his life. The greater the empathic capacity of the individual, the greater his capacity to vote and otherwise participate effectively in the life of a modern state.

FRUSTRATION–AGGRESSION

Drives, as suggested earlier, are releases of "psychic energy" designed to satisfy an individual's more pressing needs. When drives fail to adequately satisfy the individual's need or needs, the individual becomes so uncomfortable and anxious that the elimination or reduction of frustration becomes an end in itself, *regardless of its cause or causes.*[33] A man may beat his dog to let off steam because of an unsatisfactory but unalterable job situation. Kicking the dog does not modify the source of frustration, but it does offer temporary relief. In a similar vein, Allport speaks of "*scapegoating* and *free-floating frustration.*"[34] Scapegoating, like kicking the dog, refers to venting frustration due to one's own inadequacies and failures on weaker groups in the society. Thus Allport suggests that the excessive racial prejudice of the poor southern white represents a subconscious effort by the poor white to relieve frustrations generated by his own marginal situation and to salve his ego by assuring his superiority over at least one segment of society.

Free-floating frustration refers to the hypothesis that frustration caused by the deprivation of one or more needs is fluid, and that regardless of its source, frustration will be reduced through whatever channel is available—be it sublimination, aggression, or one of the other defense mechanisms discussed earlier.

The frequency with which pent-up frustrations find outlets in the form of aggressive behavior has led to the formulation of a frustration–aggression hypothesis: the greater the source of unresolved frustration in an individual or collection of individuals, including nations, the greater the likelihood that such individuals will mainfest aggressive behavior. This does not mean that all frustration automatically leads to aggression. Much is displaced cathartically or through other mechanisms such as sublimination or fantasy. The frustration–aggression hypothesis suggests that in seeking the causes of aggressive behavior (ranging from suicide and urban riots through international conflict), one would be well advised to examine the sources of frustration in the participant societies.

In applying the frustration–aggression hypothesis to an analysis of civil strife in 114 nations between 1961 and 1965, Gurr reported that levels of deprivation (frustration) were indeed significantly related to various forms of civil strife. The following passages provide some of the flavor of Gurr's analysis.

The comparative evidence on the causes of civil strife takes account of three levels of causation. The fundamental cause of civil strife is deprivation-induced discontent: The greater the discrepancy between what men believe they deserve and what they think they are capable of attaining, the greater their discontent. The more intense and widespread discontents are in a society, the more intense and widespread strife is likely to be. . . . Among the Anglo-Nordic nations, including the United States, differences in persisting deprivation—especially the deprivation associated with discrimination—are very closely related to strife; two-thirds the variation in magnitudes of strife among them is explainable by differences in the degree and extent of persisting deprivation.[35]

These findings have some general implications for explaining and resolving civil disorder in the United States. The United States has several of the conditions that in other nations lead directly the civil strife. Persisting deprivation characterized the lot of most black Americans, whatever lipservice and legal remedies have been given to equality. Repeatedly we found evidence that comparable deprivation is a chronic and all but inevitable source of strife among other nations. If the general relationship holds for the United States, then the country is likely to be afflicted by recurrent racial turmoil as long as ethnic discrimination persists. The United States also has a history of turmoil, which increases the likelihood that all Americans, white and black, will respond to discontent with demonstrative and sometimes violent behavior. Traditions of violence are unalterable in the short run; the discontents whose disruptive effects are magnified by such traditions are susceptible to change.[36]

EFFICACY

Up to this point we have viewed politics as a means of satisfying individual needs and eliminating excessive frustration. A growing body of evidence, however, suggests that certain forms of political behavior, such as high voting behavior and high levels of political trust—factors essential to the effective integration and operation of a modern state —are directly related to the positive psychological adjustment of the individual to his society.

We use the term *efficacy* to designate this additude of adjustment—the individual's feeling that he is effective, that he belongs, that he is well regarded, and that his actual behavior is congruent with his idealized self-concept.

Although psychologists have not made extensive use of the concept of *efficacy*, it has found broad acceptance among political scientists. Lane, following an extensive discussion of efficacy, proposes the following efficacy-related hypotheses:

Feelings of mastery and control over oneself and the environment, nurtured in childhood and reinforced (or inhibited) by society, tend to be generalized into a sense of political effectiveness.

A sense of political effectiveness leads people to become more alert to their political environment, more informed and partisan in their views, and more active in the political process. The person with a low sense of political efficacy is likely to live in a closed world filled with private problems.

Upper-status groups generally tend to have greater feelings of political effectiveness, generalizing from their experiences of control in private life as well as realistically appraising their greater influence. Lower-status groups tend to contrast their own power to those with upper status, thus reinforcing their feelings of social inferiority.

Negroes in Northern metropolitan areas, but not elsewhere, contrast their political power to their lesser power in other areas of life, and so achieve a relatively high sense of political efficacy.

Declining strength and vigor, and lack of occupational or family effectiveness tend to be associated with a declining sense of political effectiveness.

A sense of political effectiveness is likely to be increased by association with industry, unions, and the complexity of urban living; it is negatively related to rural life and its less dense constituencies and greater face-to-face contact with politicians.

A low sense of political efficacy may partly explain the radical view that government is operated by a remote all-powerful "Wall Street" elite.

The projection of a low sense of effectiveness upon the government may partly explain the conservative view that the government is incapable of effective action.[37]

Data presented in *The American Voter*, reflected in Lane's hypotheses, also yield persuasive arguments for the inclusion of efficacy as a significant factor in political analysis.

An important aspect of the individual's response to politics as a general area is the degree to which this response is passive in character. To some people politics is a distant and complex realm that is beyond the power of the common citizen to affect, whereas to others the affairs of government can be understood and influenced by individual citizens. We have assessed the effectiveness the individual feels in his relation to politics by using answers to several questions probing attitudes of this sort to develop a cumulative scale, on which we could array our samples. The influence this dimension of attitude has on the turnout decision is shown by Table 4–5 [not reproduced here] for the election of 1956. The rate of voting turnout was found to increase uniformly with the strength of the individual's sense of political efficacy, and more than 40 percentage points separated those whose sense was least developed from those whose sense of effectiveness was strongest.[38]

PERCEPTION, COGNITION, AND THE FORMATION OF POLITICAL ATTITUDES

Next we consider perception and cognition. As long as the human mind remains an enigmatic black box, the precise mechanics by which the brain goes about recognizing certain stimuli while ignoring others (*perception*) as well as the manner in which perceived information is categorized and sorted (*cognition*) must remain matters of conjecture. Observed social behavior as well as controlled experimentation, however, would seem to support the following propositions.[39]

First, individuals *perceive* familiar or anticipated items with greater ease than the unfamiliar. Because of his superior understanding of the criminal mind, the hero in detective stories invariably perceives what others have missed. He knows what he is looking for. Insiders smile knowingly at private jokes, while outsiders perceive only that they have missed something. The relevance of various stimuli can only be fully perceived and understood if the individual has prior information about its importance.

Second, perception is crucially influenced by what the individual wants to see or does not want to see, depending on his need states at that particular moment. When the need for food becomes excessive, for example, individuals are obsessed with the thought of food, perceiving objects in terms of food and ignoring stimuli unrelated to the hunger need. In a similar manner, most of the defense mechanisms surveyed earlier represent an attempt either to protect the ego or to gratify a psychological need by means of unconscious perceptual manipulation—that is, *selective perception.*

The most common forms of selective perception are classified as *cognitive balance* or *cognitive dissonance.* As discussed by Festinger, Cohen, and others, individuals tend inherently to maintain harmony or balance among the various elements of their thought world, including the desire to keep actual behavior in line with their idealized self-image.[40] When incoming information contradicts existing beliefs or attitudes, mental equilibrium is disturbed and harmony is replaced by dissonance. For example, if you have just purchased an automobile only to read in *Consumer Reports* that you have selected the worst possible model, the result is likely to be a certain amount of mental anguish. If you have just voted to resist school integration, yet hear from the pulpit that such behaviors is bigoted and immoral, the result is also likely to be a certain amount of dissonance. If your loyalties have always been to the Republican party, yet the evening news casts aspersions of the quality, credibility, and candor of Republican leadership, the result is again dissonance.

To prevent or reduce dissonance, individuals tend to edit out or not perceive dissonance-producing information, just as they actively select information that reinforces their existing commitments. It is not the critical evaluation in *Consumer Reports* that is studied, but the full-page ad prais-

ing your car's many virtues; not the preacher's moral con-
demnation, but the politician's righteous praise of "neigh-
borhood schools"; not the news report revealing the in-
eptitude of the Republican leadership, but the adjacent
column questioning the financial dealings of certain prominent Democrats.

When dissonance-producing stimuli cannot be ignored, the
mind has other tricks. If dissonance-producing news cannot be avoided, its source can be discredited: "The press
is controlled by the liberal establishment." Similarly, dissonance-producing behavior can be rationalized as non-
conflicting: Misrepresentation of products is not dishonesty,
just good business.

Perception refers to the admission of incoming stimuli;
cognition refers to their processing once they have arrived.
Again, we must infer how the mind processes incoming information from the overt behavior of the individual. There
appears to be broad agreement, however, on the following
points.

The vast quantities of stimuli transmitted by the sensory
organs can be effectively managed only if they are sorted
into general categories. Such sorting or categorizing provides a form of mental shorthand enabling the individual
to absorb and respond to a broad range of stimuli, with all
information relating to "blacks", for example, falling into the
same general category. Categories such as "black," "Italian,"
"Jew," and "Catholic," also contain evaluative judgments
(e.g., good, bad, neutral, safe, harmless). Thus when an incoming stimulus demands a response relating to "blacks,"
the response triggered is a standardized *attitude* summar-
izing acquired information and experiences concerning
"blacks," including an emotional evaluation of "blacks" as
good, bad, or in between. Attitudes, then, "are relatively
stable predispositions to behave or react in a certain way
toward persons, objects, institutions, or issues.[41]

Attitudes that remain tentative and readily subject to
change are generally referred to as *opinions*. When attitudes
become rigid or totally inflexible, they are referred to as
stereotypes.

How new information will be perceived and evaluated,
accordingly, depends greatly on existing attitudes. As noted
in the discussion of cognitive dissonance, information up-

setting established attitudes is poorly received and tends to be ignored, misperceived, or compartmentalized (i.e., categorized in such a way that its contradictory nature can be ignored). The more rigid or stereotyped an attitude becomes, the more resistant it is to change. The "true believers" discussed earlier are characterized by rigid cognitive structures. Their world is one of black and white. It is a world without ambiguity, where everything is good or bad, right or wrong. Information contradicting their beliefs, when it must be recognized, is merely a fraudulent trick and is best identified as such.

Concepts relating to *perception* and *cognition* address a variety of political questions. Efforts to change attitudes and persuade the masses to accept different loyalties or new ideas, whether in a political campaign in the United States or in a modernization campaign in the developing areas, clearly require the would-be change agent to do far more than make factual information available and "let truth speak for itself." To persuade people to act or to change their attitudes, the campaigner-propagandist must fit the information to the cognitive predispositions of the individuals involved. Among other things, this involves (1) getting the individual's attention, (2) penetrating his defensive mechanisms and tendencies toward cognitive balance, and (3) reinforcing existing predispositions supportive of the argument being made.

Irving L. Janis and L. Brewster Smith offer the political scientist, the political practitioner, and the propagandist a list of empirical propositions for achieving the objectives just named. The propositions cited particularly stress the need to penetrate the listener's defensive mechanisms and tendencies toward cognitive balance.

1. If, after being exposed to an impressive persuasive communication, the recipients are required to make an overt response that publicly indicates their position on the issue, the effectiveness of subsequent counteracting communications will tend to be reduced.

2. Sources regarded by the audience as prestigeful and trustworthy tend to facilitate persuasion; whereas a disesteemed source is at least temporarily a source of interference.

3. When a communicator is attempting to induce the acceptance of unpopular or counternorm images, more success will be

achieved if material highly desirable to the audience is given first, before the less desirable material, in order to build up a more favorable image of the source.

4. Under conditions where the audience is already motivated to pay attention, learning and remembering the news or informational content of a persuasive message tends to be greater if the communicator explicitly states and consistently represents his position as "neutral" rather than as a proponent or opponent of the audience's point of view.

5. Both positive and negative prestige effects tend to be lost over time: the degree to which an audience accepts persuasive statements that are attributed to a prestigeful ("respected" or "trustworthy") source tends to be comparatively high at first but gradually declines; the degree to which an audience accepts the conclusions put forth by a nonprestigeful source tends to be comparatively low at first but gradually increases.

6. When the audience is strongly opposed to the position advocated by the communicator, it is generaly more effective to discuss the opposing arguments than to present only the arguments in favor of one side of the issue.

7. Even when the audience is not initially opposed to the communicator's position, a two-sided presentation will be more effective in creating sustained changes in images than a one-sided presentation, if the communication is given under conditions where the audience will subsequently be exposed to countercommunications (which present the opposing arguments.)[42]

DECISION MAKING

The area of decision making represents a second and equally important application of the concepts related to perception and cognition. Political scientists have pursued three principal approaches to the subject: a rational approach, an environmental approach, and an idiosyncratic approach. The rational approach, discussed in Chapter 5 contends that important political decisions are actually group decisions and that the irrationality of any one decision maker will generally be corrected by those around him. The rational approach might also suggest that voters, judged in historical perspective, usually make the best choice. In both instances, the rational approach suggests that psychological factors at the individual level cancel each other out at the group level.

The environmental approach, characterized by the foreign policy decision model of Snyder, Bruck, and Sapin (see Figure 6.2), while allowing for the influence of personality, suggests that decisions are largely forced on the individual, whose decisions reflect the balancing of the diverse group, institutional, international, and ideological pressures to which he is subjected.[43]

The environmental model is of considerable utility in out-

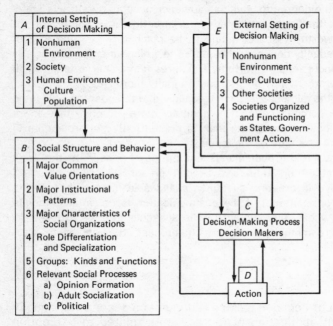

State "X" as Actor in a Situation

(Situation is comprised of a combination of selectively relevant factors in the external and internal setting as interpreted by the decision makers.)

Figure 6.2 State *X* as actor in a situation comprised of a combination of selectively relevant factors in the external and internal setting as interpreted by the decision makers. (R. C. Snyder, R. W. Bruck, and B. Sapin, eds., *Foreign Policy Decision Making.* Copyright © 1962 by The Free Press of Glencoe, A Division of The Macmillan Company; reprinted by permission of the publisher.)

lining the types of pressure decision makers are subjected to. And, providing a preponderance of the pressures are pushing in the same direction, the environmental model predicts with fair accuracy the decisions that are likely to be made under different contingencies.

The idiosyncratic approach to decision making, drawing on the concepts of *perception* and *cognition* as well as the full array of *need* and *ego* concepts discussed earlier, stresses the inherent capacity of the human mind for irrational behavior. In answer to the rationalist's suggestion that personality idiosyncrasies are "canceled" by the group, personality analysts cite examples such as the bizarre and idiosyncratic decisions made by Hitler during World War II, in direct contradiction to the counsel of his military advisors. They might also cite Franklin Roosevelt's fatal trust and confidence in Stalin, or Woodrow Wilson's "ego commitment" to the League of Nations and the Treaty of Versailles.

In responding to the environmental model, proponents of the idiosyncratic approach suggest that the pressures on decision makers are usually vague, ambiguous, and shifting, rather than uniform, and that the manner in which the decision maker responds to varying pressures depends to a large extent on how he *perceives* them.

To use a simple analogy, picture a typical American viewing a football game on television, when suddenly flames burst through the wall. Quite obviously, the individual will think "fire." Now picture a less obvious situation in which the flames do not burst through the wall, but the temperature suddenly goes up 5, or 10 or 15 degrees. Does the individual yell "fire"? Does he open the window or take off his shirt? Does he turn down the thermostat? Or does he ignore the situation, hoping it will go away until after the game?

The climate of most political decisions, proponents of the idiosyncratic approach would argue, is much closer to ambiguous changes in temperature than to flames bursting through the wall.

As general propositions, Fred I. Greenstein and other advocates of the idiosyncratic approach suggest that the greater the degree of ambiguity present in a situation, the greater the autonomy of the decision maker, and the greater the "rush" or time factor, the greater the likelihood that personality factors will influence the outcome of the decision.[44]

In stressing the role of personality factors on political behavior, Greenstein is careful to caution that some issues may be more psychologically loaded than others:

Certain types of environmental stimuli undoubtedly have a greater "resonance" with the deeper layers of the personality than do others. These are the stimuli which evoke "disproportionately" emotional responses—people seem to be "oversensitive" to them. They are stimuli which politicians learn to be wary of—for example, such issues as capital punishment, cruelty to animals, and, in recent years, fluoridation of drinking water. Often their stimulus value may be to only a rather small segment of the electorate, but their capacity to arouse fervid response may be such that a Congressman would prefer to confront his constituents on such knotty matters as revision of the tariff affecting the district's principal industry than on, in the phrase of the authors of *Voting*, a "style issue" such as humane slaughtering.[45]

OPERANT CONDITIONING AS AN
APPROACH TO POLITICAL LEARNING

When a hungry rat accidently presses a lever and receives a pellet of food as a reward, one aspect of its random behavior has been reinforced. With continued repetition of the sequence, the rat begins to associate pressing the lever with the acquisition of food, and it goes directly to the lever whenever it wants to be fed, Specifically, the rat has *learned* to associate the lever with food.

From the perspective of the experimenter, the rat has been *operantly conditioned* to associate the lever with food. That is, by the purposeful use of reinforcement, the experimenter has taught the rat to associate the lever with food.[46]

In earlier discussions of socialization and attitude formation, we used such concepts as *identification* to explain the process by which the child acquires his political loyalties and learns to relate to his political environment. Proponents believe that operant conditioning is a far more efficient means of studying political learning than the use of concepts such as *identification*, which cannot be directly observed and which go far beyond the limits of what can be inferred by observing how individuals respond to certain stimuli.[47] This point can be illustrated by placing the two approaches side by side.

Hess and Torney suggest that the phenomenon that "children tend to adopt the party of their parents when both parents are members of the same party" can best be explained by the "identification model"—that is, by the inference that the child, by identifying with his parents, makes their political loyalties his own.[48] (The mechanics of the identification process were discussed on pp. 147–148.)

Advocates of the operant conditioning approach to socialization alternately suggest that when the child randomly copies statements by his parents to the effect that "Republicans were good or that Democrats were bad," he will be reinforced by smiles, laughter, or pats on the head. As such reinforcement continues over time, the child is said to learn to associate being Republican with positive reinforcement and to accept being Republican as the best means of gratifying his immediate needs for parental affection. In the absence of conflicting stimuli in the future years, it is probable that this initial predisposition or "attitude" toward Republicanism will continue to be in force.

On the surface, at least, the operant conditioning approach to political learning appears to have the advantages of simplicity and ease of operationalization. It is much easier to question children about the type of reinforcement they have received in regard to certain political questions than to ascertain the extent of their identification with their parents. Furthermore, the operant conditioning approach also lends itself more readily to experimental research. Subjects can be operantly conditioned under the controlled circumstances of the small group laboratory; it is doubtful, however, whether the political manifestations of the identification process could be so readily managed.

Proponents of operant conditioning also argue that operant conditioning is the most efficient means of treating all learned political behavior. Nationalism, for example, might be analyzed in terms of the extent to which positive responses toward the nation and its symbols were reinforced by parents, teachers, and peers, as opposed to the extent that the symbols of the family, faith, or religious group were favored over the nation.

If *identification* and *operant conditioning* explain political learning equally well, and if operant conditioning is easier to operationalize and easier to examine empirically both in survey research and in the controlled circumstances of the laboratory, there is little apparent utility in continuing to use such terms as *identification* as explanatory concepts in political research.

Two factors, however, mitigate against wholly adopting the more manageable and empirically testable process of operant conditioning as a means of studying political learning and the acquisition of political attitudes. First, although operant conditioning is intuitively appealing, relatively few political or social researchers have utilized the technique; thus we lack a balanced evaluation of its strengths and weaknesses. This is not to criticize the technique, but rather to question the reluctance of political scientists to employ an approach that was clearly demonstrated to be politically relevant by the noted British psychologist H. J. Eysenck as early as 1954.[49] There is little doubt that in the years to come operant conditioning will be a predominant method of examining the way in which people learn political attitudes.

A more direct argument for the continued use of concepts such as identification (i.e., concepts that rely on a weak empirical base) is that they explain more than the mere learning of political preferences. Operant conditioning is useful in explaining the acquisition of attitudes, but the technique offers little help in elucidating the intense emotional attachment that frequently accompanies the identification of an individual with his nation or party, or with a charismatic leader. How, specifically, do individuals acquire the emotional intensity that underlies so many of their attitudes?

In 1954 Eysenck suggested that the problem of attitude intensity could be represented by the formula

(6.1) $$s^E r = s^H r \times D$$

Where $s^E r$ is reaction potential; $s^H r$ is habit/attitude (Eysenck had earlier demonstrated the similarity between attitudes and habits), and D represents motivation or drives.[50]

Thus attitude intensity or "reaction potential" is the product of attitudes times drives. The more intensely an individual's needs are linked to a particular attitude structure, the more intensely he can be expected to respond. Again, it seems that Eysenck's formulation of attitude intensity could be more readily subjected to the controlled observation than similar formulations based on less tangible concepts. Given the present lack of research, however, statements on the subject must remain inconclusive.

CRITIQUE: PSYCHOLOGY AND POLITICS

The relevance of psychological concepts to the study of politics is beyond question. Their use, however, is not without severe problems.

The first set of problems relates to the psychological concepts themselves. Probably the greatest shock awaiting the political scientist who ventures into the realm of psychology is that the vocabulary of the social and clinical psychologist rivals that of the political scientist in imprecision and ambiguity. We noted earlier that "personality" is reputed to have some 400 definitions, with many widely accepted definitions referring to personality vaguely as the collection of an individual's characteristics, habits, traits, idiosyncrasies, and so on, and the interrelations among them. *Identification, projection,* and *self* have numerous meanings in addition to the definitions provided in the preceding discussion. The same is true of virtually all concepts covered in this chapter.

It is also important to realize that psychologists disagree intensely regarding the process by which external stimuli are influenced by personality variables, and the extent of such influence. At one extreme fall the neobehaviorists of the Skinnerian school who largely ignore the existence of personality. To the disciples of B. F. Skinner, the nervous system is a largely mechanical affair that receives stimuli from the environment and triggers the appropriate response mechanism. Learning is primarily a matter of operant conditioning—of reinforcing the responses that bring the greatest amount of pleasure or least amount of pain, depending on the situation.[51]

At the opposite end of the scale fall the psychoanalysts and some clinical psychologists. If the Skinnerians see the human mind as a black box, unfathomable by the techniques of modern science, the psychoanalysts have filled that box with a host of items, mostly unconscious, including self-concepts, defense mechanisms, an ego, a super-ego, a libido, and an id, all of which cannot be directly observed.

When the psychologist uses terms such as ego, super ego, self concept, and self-ideal, he is saying (1) that the ways human beings react to different situations suggest that nonobservable mental process occur, and (2) that acting as if these processes occur facilitates our ability to predict and explain human behavior.

However, there is a growing feeling among psychologists in all fields that the psychoanalytic concepts of id, ego, and super-ego do not really aid in the prediction and explanation of human behavior. Their argument is both simple and logical. If the existence of subconscious mechanisms can be inferred only by observing how individuals respond to certain stimuli, it is sufficient to say that certain specified stimuli lead to certain specified responses under certain specified conditions—a testable proposition. Going beyond the observable data and inventing untestable categories within the subconscious merely confuses matters.

Debate also exists over the use of concepts such as self, identification, and frustration–aggression. Eysenck has suggested that the concepts of identification, self, and frustration–aggression, like those of ego, id, and super-ego, add little to the psychologist's analytic ability to predict and explain. This view is not shared by large numbers of psychologists, however. The political scientist is thus best left with the understanding that the utility of many psychological concepts used by political scientists are currently the subject of debate and reevaluation.

A second set of problems involves the use of psychological concepts by political scientists. Without citing examples, we can mention that political scientists working with psychological variables have frequently been guilty of *reductionism* or *psychologizing* (e.g., reducing all political events to psychological explanations). As stressed in the opening of this chapter, political behavior is generally the result of the interaction of a variety of factors, and some of them may be psychological. The challenge psychology presents to the political scientist is not to explain all of politics in terms of psychology, but to determine under what circumstances psychological variables may be relevant, and if relevant, how they "fit" with other variables to explain the total picture.

Unlike Harold Lasswell, the founder of political psychology, few political scientists have received extensive training in the field of psychology. Psychological concepts are extremely difficult to interpret, operationalize, and measure, and to apply them loosely does a profound disservice to both the psychologist and the political scientist.

Turning to a third set of problems, we note that many psychological concepts discussed in this chapter have been developed and tested on the basis of highly controlled individual and small group experiments. A considerable "inferential leap" is involved in postulating that large populations operating in the real world will behave just like a few individuals laboring under a unique and highly controlled environment. The distance between the laboratory and the real world is sometimes exceedingly great. This is not to suggest that the leap should not be made, however, for perhaps the most pressing need confronting political science today is for tightly controlled experiments capable of giving anchor to our rather heady theories.

Fourth, many psychological constructs are the product of definite Western bias. Several anthropologists have remarked that the *ego* functions of individuals reared in traditional areas of Africa or Asia appear to be either different from or less developed than those of Western man. Also, as noted elsewhere in this chapter, psychological needs vary in quality and in quantity, and means of gratification vary from one culture to another. Responses to pschological tests also vary from one country to another. What may be judged as a paranoiac response in the United States might be an entirely realistic reaction in certain areas of Africa. Such cultural variations have not always been considered in cross-national comparisons, and they are extremely difficult to measure.

In sum, it might be suggested that the application of psychological concepts to political analysis be viewed as a new horizon, filled with promise but necessarily approached with caution.

NOTES

[1] J. Milton Yinger, *Toward a Field Theory of Behavior* (New York: McGraw-Hill, 1965).

[2] Kenneth J. Gergen, *The Concept of Self* (New York: Holt, Rinehart & Winston, 1971); Orrin E. Klapp, *Collective Search for Identity* (New York: Holt, Rinehart & Winston, 1969).

[3] Charles Horton Cooley, *Human Nature and the Social Order* (New York: Scribner's, 1902), pp. 184–185.

[4] Abraham H. Maslow, *Motivation and Personality*, 2nd ed. (New York: Harper & Row, 1970); James C. Coleman, *Personality Dynamics and Effective Behavior* (Glenview, Ill.: Scott, Foresman, 1960).

[5] Harry F. Harlow, "Mice, Monkeys, Men, and Motives," *Psychological Review*, vol. 60 (1953), pp. 23–32.

[6] James C. Coleman, *Personality Dynamics and Effective Behavior*, pp. 125–129.

[7] William F. Fey, "Correlates of Certain Subjective Attitudes Toward Self and Others," *Journal of Clinical Psychiatry*, vol. 13 (1957), p. 45.

[8] C. D. Spielberger, ed., *Anxiety and Behavior* (New York: Academic Press, 1966).

[9] James C. Coleman, *Personality Dynamics and Effective Behavior*, pp. 126–129.

[10] David C. McClelland, *The Achieving Society* (New York: Van Nostrand Reinhold, 1961), pp. 63–106.

[11] Donald B. Lindsley, "Psychophysiology and Motivation," in Robert J. C. Harper, Charles C. Anderson, Clifford I. Christensen, and Steven M. Hunka, eds., *The Cognitive Process: Readings* (Englewood Cliffs, N.J.: Prentice-Hall, 1964), pp. 56–57; Albert Mehrabian, *An Analysis of Personality Theories* (Englewood Cliffs, N.J.: Prentice-Hall, 1968).

[12] William C. Menninger, *Psychiatry: Its Evolution and Present Status* (Ithaca, N.Y.: Cornell University Press, 1948), pp. 73–74.

[13] Ibid., p. 75.

[14] Robert E. Lane, *Political Thinking and Consciousness* (Chicago: Markham, 1969), pp. 143–144.

[15] T. W. Adorno, Else Frenkel-Brunswek, Daniel J. Levinson, and R. Nevitt Sanford, *The Authoritarian Personality* (New York: Harper & Row, 1964).

[16] Ibid., p. 228.

[17] J. P. Kitscht and R. C. Dillehay, *Dimensions of Authoritarianism: A Review of Research and Theory* (Lexington: University of Kentucky Press, 1967).

[18] Herbert McCloskey, "Conservatism and Personality," *American Political Science Review*, vol. 52 (March 1958), pp. 35, 37.

[19] Gabriel A. Almond, *The Appeals of Communism* (Princeton, N.J.: Princeton University Press, 1954), pp. 279, 280. Copyright 1954 by Princeton University Press; reprinted by permission of the publisher.

[20] Gordon W. Allport, *The Nature of Prejudice* (Reading, Mass.: Addison-Wesley, 1954), pp. 372–374.

[21] Hans Gerth, "The Nazi Party: Its Leadership and Composition," *American Journal of Sociology*, vol. 45 (January 1940), pp. 526–527.

[22] Harold Lasswell, "The Psychology of Hitlerism," *Political Quarterly*, vol. 4, no. 3 (July–September, 1933), p. 378.

[23] Gordon W. Allport, *The Nature of Prejudice*, chaps. 15, 21; George Eaton Simpson and J. Milton Yinger, *Racial and Cultural Minorities*, 3rd ed. (New York: Harper & Row, 1965), pp. 52–63.

[24] Erik H. Erikson, *Identity: Youth and Crisis* (New York: Norton, 1968); Orrin E. Klapp, *Collective Search for Identity*.

[25] Jerome Kagan, "The Concept of Identification," *The Psychological Review*, vol. 65 (September 1958), pp. 296–305; R. N. Sanford, "The

Dynamics of Identification," *The Psychological Review*, vol. 62 (1955), pp. 106–118; Kenneth J. Gergen, *The Concept of Self.*

[26] David Easton and Jack Dennis, *Children in the Political System: Origins of Political Legitimacy* (New York: McGraw-Hill, 1969), p. 372.

[27] Robert D. Hess and Judith V. Torney, *The Development of Political Attitudes in Children* (Chicago: Aldine, 1967), p. 217.

[28] Gabriel A. Almond, *The Appeals of Communism*, p. 272. Copyright 1954 by Princeton University Press; reprinted by permission of the publisher.

[29] Colin M. Turnbull, *The Lonely African* (Garden City, N.Y.: Doubleday, Anchor Books, 1962), p. 147.

[30] Leonard W. Doob, *Patriotism and Nationalism* (New Haven, Conn.: Yale University Press, 1964).

[31] Daniel Lerner, *The Passing of Traditional Society* (New York: Free Press, 1958), pp. 49–50.

[32] Ibid., pp. 24–25.

[33] Leonard Berkowitz, *Aggression: A Social Psychological Analysis* (New York: McGraw-Hill, 1962), pp. 27–50.

[34] Gordon W. Allport, *The Nature of Prejudice*, chaps. 15, 21.

[35] Ted Robert Gurr, "A Comparative Study of Civil Strife," in Hugh Davis Graham and Ted Robert Gurr, eds., *Violence in America* (New York: Bantam, 1970), pp. 620–621.

[36] Ibid., p. 623.

[37] Robert E. Lane, *Political Life* (New York: Free Press, 1959), pp. 154–155.

[38] Angus Campbell, Phillip E. Converse, Warren E. Miller, and Donald E. Stokes, *The American Voter* (New York: Wiley, 1960), pp. 104–105.

[39] For a general review, see Robert J. C. Harper et al., eds., *The Cognitive Process: Readings.*

[40] Leon Festinger, *A Theory of Cognitive Dissonance* (Evanston, Ill.: Row, Peterson, 1957); Arthur R. Cohen, *Attitude Change and Social Influence* (New York: Basic Books, 1964).

[41] J. P. Chaplin, *Dictionary of Psychology* (New York: Dell, 1968), p. 42.

[42] Irving L. Janis and L. Brewster Smith, "Effects of Education and Persuasion on National and International Images," in Herbert C. Kelman, ed., *International Behavior: A Social-Psychological Analysis.* Copyright © 1965 by Holt, Rinehart & Winston; reprinted by permission of the publisher. Pp. 219–225.

[43] Richard C. Snyder, R. W. Bruck and Burton Sapin, eds., *Foreign Policy Decision Making* (New York: Free Press, 1962).

[44] Fred I. Greenstein, "The Impact of Personality on Politics: An Attempt to Clear Away Underbrush," *American Political Science Review*, vol. 61 (September 1967), pp. 629–641. Also see Fred I. Greenstein, *Personality and Politics* (Chicago: Markham, 1969).

[45] Greenstein, "The Impact of Personality," p. 640.

[46] For a general review see: G. Cutonia, ed., *Contemporary Research in Operant Behavior* (Glenview, Ill.: Scott, Foresman, 1968).

[47] James W. Dyson, "The Outmoded Zeitgeist of Political Socialization and Political Attitude Research," paper presented at the Southern Political Science Association Meetings in Gatlinburg, November 1971.

[48] Hess and Torney, *The Development of Political Attitudes in Children*, p. 217.

[49] H. J. Eysenck, *The Psychology of Politics* (London: Routledge & Kegan Paul, 1954).

[50] Ibid., p. 249.

[51] Representative of B. F. Skinner's works are *The Behavior of Organisms* (New York: Appleton-Century-Crofts, 1961), *Walden Two* (New York: Macmillan, 1948), *Science and Human Behavior* (New York: Macmillan, 1953), and *Beyond Freedom and Dignity* (New York: Knopf, 1971).

Index

A

Access, 49
Adams, John Q., 130
Adaptation (function), 62
Adorno, et al., 144
Affectivity, 88
Africa, 15
Alienation, 5, 15
Allport, Gordon, 154
Almond, Gabriel A., 22, 64, 96, 97, 98, 102, 145
American Voter, The, 157
Analytical frameworks, 9
Anthropology, 75, 76
Anti-intraception, 3
Apter, David E., 84, 85, 91, 92
Aristotle, 6, 115
Arrow, Kenneth, 111
Ascription, 89
Ashanti, 84
Asia, 15
Attitude, 159
Authoritarian personality, 143, 144
Authorities, 20
Authority, 5, 31
Axelrod, Robert, 131

B

Bachrach, Peter, 17
Bales, Robert F., 52
Bangla-Desh, 58
Baratz, M. S., 29
Bargaining, 31, 106, 107, 119, 120, 122, 123
Barnouw Victor, 93

Beard, Charles A., 56
Behaviorists, 15
Bentley, Arthur F., 48
Biafra, 58
Biddle, Bruce J., 45
Black Panther Party, 49
Boulding, Kenneth, 126
Bowles, Hargrove, 115
Britain, 50
Bruck, R. W., 162
Buchanan, James M., 129
Butalanffy, Ludwig van, 9

C

Capacity, 91
Cartwright, Darwin, 31, 52
Catagna, Albert C., 93, 100, 101
Causality, 16
Change, 5
Clay, Henry, 130
Coalition formation, 106, 107, 123
Cognition, 157, 159, 160, 163
Cognitive balance, 158
Cognitive dissonance, 158
Cohen, Arthur, 158
Cohesion, 49
Coleman, James S., 111
Collective orientation, 88
Committee for Comparative Politics of the Social Science Research Council, 57
Communications, 33, 34, 35, 36, 37, 38, 39, 40, 41, 66
Communist Party, 145
Competition, 31

Concept, 4, 5, 11
Conceptual definition, 12
Conceptual frameworks, 4, 5, 9, 11
Conflict, 31, 127, 128
Congress, 27
Constitutional law, 17
Construct, 6
Conventionalism, 143
Cooley, Charles Horton, 139
Cooperation, 31, 127, 128, 129
Cost, 106, 107, 118, 119
Cultural lag, 85
Cultural relativity, 15
Culture, 13, 92, 94, 95, 103
Currencies, 116

D
Dahl, Robert A., 27, 28, 29, 31, 33, 56, 113, 116, 118, 120
Decision making, 1, 40, 107, 112, 161
Deductive theory, 8
Defense mechanisms, 141, 167
Demands, 20
Dennis, Jack, 148
Deutsch, Karl W., 25, 35, 40, 116
Development, 5, 90, 101, 102
Devine, Donald J., 99
Differentiation, 91
Diffuse, 89
Disintegration, 92
Displacement, 141
Distribution, 58
Domhoff, William, 56
Doob, Leonard W., 151, 153
Downs, Anthony, 8, 9, 108, 131
Drives, 139, 140, 154
Dye, Thomas R., 55
Dyson, James W., 54

E
Easton, David, 20, 21, 22, 23, 148
Eclectic functionalism, 59, 60
Economic class, 12
Economics, 1, 106
Efficacy, 156, 157
Ego, 9, 139, 141, 163, 167, 169
Elazer, Daniel J., 99
Elitism, 29, 30, 56
Empathy, 152, 153
Empirical concept, 5

Empirical functionalism, 59, 60
Empirical theory, 11
Equality, 91
Equilibrium, 63
Ethiopia, 67
Europe, 40
European Economic Community, 23, 50
Evans-Pritchard, E. E., 84
Exchange, 116
Eysenck, H. J., 166, 168

F
Feedback, 20, 22, 37
Festinger, Leon, 158
Fiduciary, 121
Field, 137
Flanagan, William, 59
Fogelman, Edwin, 59
Fortes, 84
Free-floating frustration, 154
Freud, Sigmund, 6
Froman, Lewis A., Jr., 50
Frustration-aggression hypothesis, 154
Function, 59, 70

G
Gain, 38
Game theory, 106, 107, 125, 126, 127, 128, 129, 130
Gatekeepers, 21
Gemeinschaft, 87
Gerth, Hans, 146, 147
Gesellschaft, 87
Goal attainment, 62
Goldberg, Arthur, 112
Golembiewski, Robert, 11
Greenstein, Fred I., 163, 164
Groups, 48, 50, 51
Gurr, R. T., 155

H
Hagen, Everett E., 83
Herskowits, Melville J., 76
Hess, Robert D., 149, 165, 172
Heuristic concept, 5
Hindu society, 63
Hitler, 163
Hobbes, Thomas, 6, 7, 81
Huitt, Ralph H., 47

Hunter, Floyd, 56
Huntington, Samuel P., 92
Hypothesis, 4, 5, 6, 7, 11

I
Id, 6, 9, 167
Idealized self-concept, 140
Identification, 148, 164, 165, 166, 167
Identity, 57, 139
Identity crisis, 147
Indian caste system, 63
Inductive theory, 8
Influence, 5, 31
Inkeles, Alex, 55
Input functions, 65
Integration, 62, 151
Interdependence (functional), 63
Interest aggregation, 65, 66
Interest articulation, 65
Interest groups, 50
International law, 17
International relations, 17

J
Jaquaribe, Helio, 92
Janis, Irving L., 160, 161
John Birch Society, 49

K
Kaplan, Morton A., 31
Kennan, George F., 37
Khedouri, Elie, 85
Klockholn, Clyde, 93
Kroeber, Alfred, 93, 119
Kuhn, Alfred, 27

L
Lag, 38, 39
Lane, Robert E., 142, 143, 156, 157
Lasswell, Harold, 31, 146, 147, 168
Latent functions, 60
Lead, 38, 39
Leadership, 31
League of Nations, 163
Learning theory, 1
Lebanon, 85
Legislative behavior, 47
Legitimacy, 57
Lerner, Daniel, 152, 153
Leveling devices, 80
Leviathan, 7

Levy, Marion J., Jr., 11, 61
Lewis, Oscar, 86
Libido, 167
Lieber, Robert J., 50
Linblom, Charles, 116, 118, 120
Lippitt, Ronald, 53
Lipset, Seymour Martin, 55
Lipsky, Michael, 114
Load, 38
Locke, John, 115
Logoli, 77
Looking-glass self, 139
Low-range theory, 9

M
McClelland, David C., 15, 34
McClosky, H., 144
McGovern, George, 46
Maddox, Lester, 47
Malthus, Thomas, 115
Manifest functions, 60
Marx, Karl, 55
Marxism, 95
Mathews, Donald R., 47
Mead, Margaret, 92, 93
Merton, Robert K., 60
Metaphysical concepts, 5
Middle-range theory, 9
Mills, C. Wright, 56
Minimax strategy, 129
Models, 4, 5, 10, 11
Modern, 101, 102
Modernization, 90
Modernizing, 101, 102
Moore, Sir Thomas, 6
Mores, 138
Morgenthau, Hans J., 25, 99

N
NAACP, 51
Nagel, Jack J., 27, 28, 30, 31
Nash, Manning, 77, 80, 100
National character, 99, 100, 101, 102
Nationalism, 151, 152, 153
Natural law, 6
Need, 39, 41, 163
Need disequilibrium, 146
Need state, 140
Neustadt, Richard, 32
Nixon, Richard, 4
Nkrumah, Kwame, 84

Normative theories, 7
Norms, 45, 138
Nuer, 77

O
Ogborn, William F., 85
Olsen, Mancur, Jr., 108
Operant conditioning, 164, 165, 166
Operational definition, 12
Operationalization, 12, 13
Opinion, 159
Opportunity costs, 118, 119
Output functions, 65

P
Parochial culture, 97
Parochial-participant (culture), 97
Parson, Talcott, 83, 87, 88, 90, 92, 98, 101
Participant political cultures, 97
Participation, 57
Particularistic, 88
Patron, 80
Pattern maintenance (function), 62
Peasants, 77, 78, 81, 101
Penetration, 57
Perception, 157–160, 163
Personality, 1, 13
Plato, 6, 115
Plotnicov, Leonard, 86
Pluralism, 27, 56
Political community, 20
Political culture, 95, 96, 97, 99, 101
Political integration, 57
Political science, 75
Political socialization and recruitment, 65
Political theory, 6
Political thought, 17
Power, 2, 5, 14, 28–31, 33, 35
Presidential power, 32
Presidential roles, 47
Primitive societies, 76
Projection, 141, 144
Psychologizing, 168
Public administration, 17, 53
Pye, Lucian, 91, 99

R
Rapoport, 11
Rationality, 107, 112

Rationalization, 141
Reductionism, 168
Regime, 20
Regulation of exchange, 116, 117
Reintegration, 92
Replicability, 2
Resource, 106, 107, 113, 114, 115
Riker, William H., 10, 112, 124, 130
Rivalry, 31
Role, 45, 69, 71
Role content, 45
Role cues, 147
Roosevelt, Franklin, 163
Ross, Robert L., 50
Rule adjudication, 66
Rule application, 66
Rule making, 66

S
Sapin, Burton, 162
Scapegoating, 147, 154
Schelling, Thomas C., 120, 121
Scientific method, 2
Selective perception, 158
Self-actualization, 140
Self-concept, 139, 167
Self-needs, 139
Self-oriented, 88
Sensory data, 2
Shapiro, Michael, 132
Shils, Edward A., 88, 101
Sjøberg, Gideon, 80
Skinner, B. F., 167
Small group, 51, 52
Smith, Adam, 115
Smith, L. Brewster, 160, 161
Snyder, Richard C., 162
Social class, 12
Social stratification, 54, 58
Social structure, 44
Socialization, 1, 53, 148, 149
Society for General Systems Research, 19
Sociology, 44
Soviet Union, 37, 54, 66, 67
Spatial models, 131, 132
Specialization, 91
Specificity, 89
Spectator, 122
Stalin, Joseph, 163
Stefanaconi, 82

Stereotype, 144, 159, 160
Structural functional analysis, 59, 61, 66, 67, 68, 69
Subject participant (culture), 97
Super-ego, 6, 9, 139, 141, 167
Supports, 20, 21
Supreme Court, 59
Systems analysis, 10, 19, 24

T
Tallensi, 77
Theories, 4, 5, 6, 9, 11
Thomas, Edwin J., 45
Third World, 75
Tonnies, F., 87, 90
Torney, Judith V., 149, 165
Traditional societies, 82, 83, 101
Transfer, 148
Treaty of Versailles, 163
True believers, 150, 160
Truman, David B., 49, 50, 56
Tullock, Gordon, 129
Turnbull, Colin, 150, 151

U
United States Senate, 47, 52
Universality, 88
Utility, 109, 110, 111

V
Verba, Sidney M., 22, 54, 97, 98, 99
Vietnam, 4, 38

W
Wade, L. L., 121
Wahlke, John C., 47
Wallace, George C., 46
Weber, Max, 87, 90
Weiner, Myron, 91
White, Ralph K., 53
Wilson, Woodrow, 163
World War II, 75
Wolf, Eric R., 78

Y
Yinger, J. Milton, 137, 138
Young Americans for Freedom, 48
Young Socialist Alliance, 48
Youth, 48

Z
Zander, Alvin, 52
Zavoina, William, 10, 112
Zeigler, Harmon, 55

DATE DUE